*Won by One*

OTHER BOOKS OF BARRY BLACKSTONE

*Though None Go With Me*
*Rendezvous in Paris*
*Though One Go With Me*
*Scotland Journey*
*The Region Beyond*
*Enlarge My Coast*
*From Dan to Beersheba and Beyond*
*The Uttermost Part*
*Homestead Homilies*
*Rover: A Boy's Best Friend*
*North to Alaska and Back*
*Another Day in Nazareth*
*Sermonettes from the Seashore*
*Earth's Farthest Bounds*
*Angling Admonitions*
*Beyond the Bend*
*Expendable*
*Meows from the Manse*
*At a Moment's Notice*
*Reaching the Unreached*
*Satan's Super Soldiers*
*Threescore and Ten*

# Won by One

*by*
BARRY BLACKSTONE

RESOURCE *Publications* · Eugene, Oregon

WON BY ONE

Copyright © 2025 Barry Blackstone. All rights reserved. Except for brief quotations in critical publications or reviews, no part of this book may be reproduced in any manner without prior written permission from the publisher. Write: Permissions, Wipf and Stock Publishers, 199 W. 8th Ave., Suite 3, Eugene, OR 97401.

Resource Publications
An Imprint of Wipf and Stock Publishers
199 W. 8th Ave., Suite 3
Eugene, OR 97401

www.wipfandstock.com

PAPERBACK ISBN: 979-8-3852-4665-6
HARDCOVER ISBN: 979-8-3852-4666-3
EBOOK ISBN: 979-8-3852-4667-0

VERSION NUMBER 06/04/25

I dedicate this devotional to one of the best soul-winners I have had the privilege to know: Michael Davis, and to the many others who will not meet their Saviour empty-handed!

# Contents

Won by One | 1

1. **WON:** Abram the Hebrew—**BY:** Genesis 15:6—**ONE:** God | 5
2. **WON:** Shem the Semite—**BY:** Hebrews 11:7—**ONE:** Noah | 9
3. **WON:** Gaius the Roman—**BY:** III John 1, 4—**ONE:** John | 13
4. **WON:** The Samaritan Woman—**BY:** John 4:29—**ONE:** Jesus | 17
5. **WON:** Titus the Greek—**BY:** Titus 1:4—**ONE:** Paul | 21
6. **WON:** Ittai the Gittite—**BY:** II Samuel 15:21—**ONE:** David | 25
7. **WON:** Darius the Median—**BY:** Daniel 6:26—**ONE:** Daniel | 29
8. **WON:** The Ethiopian Eunuch—**BY:** Acts 8:37—**ONE:** Philip | 33
9. **WON:** Eliezer the Syrian—**BY:** Genesis 24:12 —**ONE:** Abraham | 37
10. **WON:** Bartimaeus the Blindman—**BY:** Mark 10:52 —**ONE:** Jesus | 41
11. **WON:** Ebedmelech the Ethiopian—**BY:** Jeremiah 39:18 —**ONE:** Jeremiah | 45
12. **WON:** The Philippian Jailer—**BY:** Acts 16:34—**ONE:** Paul | 49
13. **WON:** Marcus the Jew—**BY:** I Peter 5:13—**ONE:** Peter | 53
14. **WON:** Sarah the Semites—**BY:** Hebrews 11:11 —**ONE:** Abram | 57
15. **WON:** Ruth the Moabitess—**BY:** Ruth 1:16—**ONE:** Naomi | 61
16. **WON:** The Calvary Thief—**BY:** Luke 23:42—**ONE:** Jesus | 65
17. **WON:** Peter the Galilaean—**BY:** John 1:41—**ONE:** Andrew | 69
18. **WON:** Cornelius the Italian—**BY:** Acts 10:1-2—**ONE:** Peter | 73
19. **WON:** Zacchaeus the Jerichoite—**BY:** Luke 19:9 —**ONE:** Jesus | 77

20 **WON:** The Capernaum Centurian—**BY:** Matthew 8:10
—**ONE:** Jesus | 81

21 **WON:** Andrew the Fisherman—**BY:** John 1:40
—**ONE:** John the Baptist | 85

22 **WON:** Philip the Bethsaidaean—**BY:** John 1:43
—**ONE:** Jesus | 89

23 **WON:** Dionysius the Areopagite—**BY:** Acts 17:34
—**ONE:** Paul | 93

24 **WON:** The Alabaster Woman—**BY:** Luke 7:37–38
—**ONE:** Jesus | 97

25 **WON:** Hagar the Egyptian—**BY:** Genesis 16:13
—**ONE:** God | 101

26 **WON:** Nathanael the Skepic—**BY:** John 1:49—**ONE:** Philip | 105

27 **WON:** Epaenetus the Achaean—**BY:** Romans 16:5
—**ONE:** Paul | 109

28 **WON:** The Prodigal Son—**BY:** Luke 15:18—
**ONE:** The Prodigal's Father | 113

29 **WON:** Rahab the Amorite—**BY:** Hebrews 11:31
—**ONE:** God | 117

30 **WON:** Saul the Benjamite—**BY:** Acts 9:6—**ONE:** Jesus | 121

31 **WON:** Jethro the Midianite—**BY:** Exodus 18:11
—**ONE:** Moses | 125

32 **WON:** The Palsy Man—**BY:** Mark 2:5
—**ONE:** The Palsy Man's Friends | 129

33 **WON:** Uriah the Hittite—**BY:** II Samuel 11:11
—**ONE:** David | 133

34 **WON:** Nebuchadnezzar the Babylonian—
**BY:** Daniel 4:37—**ONE:** Daniel | 137

35 **WON:** Simon the Cyrenian—**BY:** Matthew 27:32
—**ONE:** Jesus | 141

36 **WON:** The Philippi Damsel—**BY:** Acts 16:18—**ONE:** Paul | 145

37 **WON:** Lydia the Thyatirian—**BY:** Acts 16:14—**ONE:** Paul | 149

38 **WON:** Simon the Canaanite—**BY:** Mark 3:18—**ONE:** Jesus | 153

39 **WON:** Zelek the Ammonite—**BY:** I Chronicles 11:39
—**ONE:** David | 157

40 **WON**: The Canaanite Woman—**BY**: Matthew 15:22
   —**ONE**: Jesus | 161

41 **WON**: Ithmah the Moabite—**BY**: I Chronicles 11:46
   —**ONE**: David | 165

42 **WON**: Mnason the Cypriote—**BY**: Acts 21:16
   —**ONE**: Barnabas | 169

43 **WON**: Ismaiah the Gibeonite—**BY**: I Chronicles 12:4
   —**ONE**: David | 173

44 **WON**: The Ninevehite King—**BY**: Jonah 3:6—**ONE**: Jonah | 177

45 **WON**: Demetrius the Christian—**BY**: III John 12
   —**ONE**: John | 181

46 **WON**: Hiram the Phoenician—**BY**: I Kings 5:7
   —**ONE**: David | 185

47 **WON**: Aristarchus the Macedonian—**BY**: Acts 19:29
   —**ONE**: Paul | 189

48 **WON**: The Rechabite Family—**BY**: Jeremiah 35:19
   —**ONE**: Elijah | 193

49 **WON**: Phebe the Cenchrean—**BY**: Romans 16:1–2
   —**ONE**: Paul | 197

50 **WON**: Tabitha the Joppaite—**BY**: Acts 9:36
   —**ONE**: Only God Knows | 201

Of All Nations | 205

# WON BY ONE

IN 2000, I STARTED research on a devotional book with the thought-provoking title that is at the head of this prelude. This nearly quarter of a century exploration started when I read Elizabeth Elliot's classic biography on her husband's death at the hands of the Auca warriors in 1956; I was five at the time. While reading of the incredible sacrifice of Jim and his four friends, I was struck for the first time with the insightful truth of Revelation 5:9 and 7:9: "And they sung a new song, saying, Thou art worthy to take the book, and to open the seals thereof: for thou wast slain, and hast redeemed us to God by thy blood out **of every kindred, and tongue, and people, and nation**. . .After this I beheld, and, lo, a great multitude, which no man could number, **of all nations, and kindreds, and people, and tongues**, stood before the throne, and before the Lamb, clothed with white robes, and palms in their hands!" Why had Jim Elliot, Roger Youderian, Ed McCully, Pete Fleming, and Nate Saint been willing to lay their lives on the line to get the Gospel to this primitive and dangerous tribal group? The simple answer implied in Elizabeth's book was so that "the Auca people would have a representative around the Throne of God on that Day!" For the first time I saw the words "all" and "every". The Church of the Living God will not fulfill the Great Commission until 'all' and 'every' is finished, and there is plenty left to reach according to those that track such things.

So you might ask why I have picked up the pen and started writing again on "Won by One". I was provoked while on my sixth short-term mission's trip to India. While visiting two former students of mine from Kerala Baptist Bible College (I have taught two different times for a month and have been asked to speak at four graduations between 2006 and 2022) from the State of Chhattisgarh where they are involved in tribal evangelism; the still small voice of the Holy Spirit told me that when I got back to the States I was to dig out the research and finish "Won by One", for I believe that the statements of the Revelation are not speaking about 'all people' but 'people from all people groups'. After this trip to Chhattisgarh and Kerala I am persuaded (Romans 14:5) that the nations have been reached, but the tribes haven't (Matthew 24:30)! **We all know salvation has been universally offered, but not universally received.** But I believe that God will before He comes after His Bride reach down through grace and mercy into the heart of at least one from all tongues, kindred, people, and nations and pluck them from Hell's fired and redeem them so on the great day of the gathering there will be not a missing tribe. I like the way Samuel Stone put it in his Church hymn, "The Church is One Foundation": *"Elect from every nation, yet one over all the earth!"* In the Church's attempt to reach 'all' (Mark 16:15), we have forgotten the 'all' we are supposed to be reaching. Somewhere in Church history we switched from the individual to the masses.

Instead of seeking the representative from every nation, we have spent our money and manpower and message to reach every individual of certain people groups to the neglect of other people groups. I like what my India friend Johnson Matthews said to me when I asked him why 10 years ago he started reaching the unreached tribal groups of the eastern mountains of central Kerala: **"Do I have the right to hear the Gospel twice when there are those who haven't heard the Gospel once!"** The other reason I have decided to write a book on this topic is the fact at the time I read Elliot's book, I was also in the midst of a series of messages to my church of a lifetime (33 years at the time of this writing) on this Biblical doctrine. The second Sunday of every months since the assemble was formed in the early 1950s has been designated Mission's Sunday. For two years (24 messages), I had been highlighting and underlining the various people groups mentioned in the Bible that had come to a saving knowledge of the Christ. My purpose and goal was to convince the people that there was one aspect of our mission outreach and our mission spending we were not involved with: trying to reach an unreached people group. We were supporting works in the Philippines, but the Philippines have been reached. We were supporting works in Brazil, but the Brazilians have been reached like the Germans, French, Korean, and Chinese. . . . ..I am not saying we stop mission outreaches to these lands, for until every creature (Mark 16:15) hears we haven't fulfilled Jesus' commission either, but what about the 2200 tribes of India alone that haven't been reached yet?

So this book comes out of those original messages, but as you see there are more than 24 chapters in this book. Over the years I have added to my list and I have expanded the Biblical examples to 50, but throughout these chapters I will be adding to the challenge as I have been challenged in the last half of my pastorate to look at the world and evangelism differently. I begin my 50th year as a pastor in a few months and I hope this book written in a devotional style will provoke the reader to get back to what I believe is the Biblical approach to evangelism: one by one! If you read through the Bible you will notice 'mass conversions' are rarely mentioned: Nineveh (Jonah 3) and Pentecost (Acts 2) are the exceptions to this observation, but individual conversions can be found in just about every book of the Bible. While conducting a nursing home service I found the words to a hymn written by C. Austin Miles with these lines: "If Christ our only King, men redeemed we strive to bring. Just one way may this be done; we must win them one by one. Side by side we stand each day, saved are we, but lost are they; they will come if we only dare, speak a word backed up by prayer. Only cowards dare refuse, dare this gift of God misuse. Ere some friends goes to his grave, speak a word his soul to save. Not for hope of great reward turn men's hearts unto the Lord. Just to see a saved man smile makes the effort well worthwhile. So you bring the one next to you, and I'll bring the one next to me; in all kinds of weather, we'll work together, and see what can be done. If you'll bring the one next to you, and I'll bring the one next to me, in no time at all, we'll have them all, so win them, and win them one by one!" When I found this song, this became the theme song if not only this devotional, but my philosophy of evangelism.

"Won by One" is just my attempt as a pastor and a preacher to revive the Church one more time to sharing the Gospel 'one by one', for I do believe we are in the 'last days' and the time is short and God still doesn't want any to perish (II Peter 3:9). My trip to India in 2022 I had a chance to share in my very first mission's conference; oh, I have preached often on the topic in my churches, but had never been asked to share in another venue. Kerala Baptist Bible College gave me that chance and in four days I spoke for 13 ½ hours on my beliefs about missions, including the theme of this book. But I came back even more focused on the importants of reaching the unreached tribes with the Gospel, but the method for them is the same as here: one by one: Christians reaching their neighbors. Once again I return to a favorite mission's hymn written by Mary Thomson: "O Zion Haste". "O Zion haste, they mission high fulfilling, to tell to all the world that God is Light; that He who made **all nations** is not willing one soul should perish, lost in shades of night. . .Proclaim to every people tongue and nation that God, in whom they live and move, is love. . .give of thy sons to bear the message glorious; give of they wealth to speed them on their way; pour out they soul for them in prayer victorious. . .!" Amen!!!!!!

# 1

## WON: ABRAM THE HEBREW
## BY: Genesis 15:6

And he believed in the LORD; and he counted it to him for righteousness.

## ONE: GOD

I BELIEVE I COULD have started this list of 'won by one' with perhaps Abel (Genesis 4:4-Hebrews 11:4) or Seth (Genesis 4:26) or Enoch (Genesis 5:21–24-Hebrews 11:5–6) or Noah (Genesis 6:8–9-Hebrews 11:7), for I believe they all came to the faith by a direct intervention of God Himself, but I chose to start with Abram because he has become the poster child of the Bible in this category and is known as 'the father of the faithful'!

    I still remember the first time I read Joshua 24:2 with an understanding heart. How shocked I was when I read: "And Joshua said unto all the people, Thus saith the LORD God of Israel, Your fathers dwelt on the other side of the flood in old time, *even* Terah, the father of Abraham, and the father of Nachor: **and they served other gods.**" Why I always thought Abraham was a believer in the One and Only, True and Living God; I don't know! Childhood Bible stories probably? But the very thought that one of my heroes of the faith worshipping 'other gods' was appalling to me, yet I would eventually come to the understanding that we all start life in some form of idolatry. And that danger continues to this day, and if not, why did John the Apostle end his first epistle this way? "Little children, keep yourselves from idols. Amen." (I John 5:21) Remember, according to Ezekiel idols are not just graven images: "Son of man, **these men have set up their idols in their heart**, and put the stumblingblock of their iniquity before their face: should I be enquired of at all by them?" (Ezekiel 14:3) Idolatry is alive and well in the 21st century, and there is still only one answer: "...believe in the LORD..."

Abram started his Biblical story a foreigner in more ways than one. Abram was actually a Babylonian from Ur of the Chaldees; certainly not a citizen of heaven: "Now therefore ye are no more strangers and foreigners, but fellowcitizens with the saints, and of the household of God." (Ephesians 2:19) Writes Paul! So how did this foreign idolater end up 'the friend of God' according to James 2:23? In Abraham (Genesis 17:5), first called Abram the Hebrew (Genesis 14:13) I see three very important precepts in Abram's story of how the Almighty God won him over: 1) **When Abram was called he obeyed**: "By faith Abraham, when he was called to go out into a place which he should after receive for an inheritance, obeyed; and he went out, not knowing whither he went." (Hebrews 11:8) Today we hear a lot about faith but very little about obedience. I learned a children's chorus as a kid that starts: ***Obedience is the very best way to show that you believe; doing exactly what the Lord commands, doing it happily...*** " I feel this is what James was trying to teach his readers when he invoked Abram and Rahab (James 2:21–26) in these classic lines: "Even so faith, if it hath not works, is dead, being alone. Yea, a man may say, Thou hast faith, and I have works: shew me thy faith without thy works, and I will shew thee my faith by my works." (James 2:17–18) Was not this the mistake of the first king of Israel: "...Behold, to obey *is* better than sacrifice...?" (I Samuel 15:22) True conversion doesn't happen without obedience! 2) **When Abram was promised he believed**: "Therefore *it is* of faith that *it might be* by grace; to the end the promise might be sure to all the seed; not to that only which is of the law, but to that also which is of the faith of Abraham; who is the father of us all." (Romans 4:16) Simply speaking, Abram took God at His Word. God's Word was enough for Abram, but few today take God at His Word! Remember, Abram took God at His Word in where he was to go, what to do when he got there, and even though "These all died in faith, not having received the promises, but having seen them afar off, and were persuaded of *them*, and embraced *them*, and confessed that they were strangers and pilgrims on the earth." (Hebrews 11:12) I remember hearing as a child: ***'God said it, I believe it, and that is good enough for me!"*** Is God's Word enough, sufficent enough for you today? 3) **When Abram was burdened he prayed**: "And as for Ishmael, I have heard thee: Behold, I have blessed him, and will make him fruitful, and will multiply him exceedingly; twelve princes shall he beget, and I will make him a great nation." (Genesis 17:20) We all know the story of Ishmael, Abram's big mistake that the world is still paying for today in the Middle East conflicts! I use this as an example that Abram was a praying man, and he was always interceding for someone (read the story of Genesis 20). If you study your Bible God's greatest men and women were prayer warriors. So what do these three characteristics have to do with God winning Abram to a saving knowledge to Himself?

Somewhere between Ur and Haran, God saw the heart of Abram. I like the way Peter put it to Cornelius: "Then Peter opened *his* mouth, and said, of a truth I perceive that God is no respecter of persons: but in every nation he that feareth him, and worketh righteousness, is accepted with him." (Acts 10:34–35) There you have what happened one day when God called Abram: "Now the LORD had said unto Abram, Get thee out of thy country, and from thy kindred, and from thy father's house, unto a land that I will shew thee." (Genesis 12:1) From our key verse printed about we are told that was the key, but to bring it full circle we must add the realization that the 'righteousness' spoken of was Jesus' righteousness: "For he hath made him *to be* sin for us, who knew no sin; that we might be made the righteousness of God in him." (II Corinthians 5:21) As I have been telling people all my life: whither Old Testament saints or New Testament saints it is the same belief: Abram looked ahead and I looked back on the redemptive work of Christ.

We should never forget that the first great evangelist was God Himself. God has never asked us to do anything that He Himself has not done? I think God won Adam and Eve to Himself after the fall! And for me you can trace the lineage of Adam and in each case it was the generation before that won the generation after with the help of God, as we are helped by the Holy Spirit of God. God has always been in the saving business: "The Lord is not slack concerning his promise, as some men count slackness; but is longsuffering to us-ward, not willing that any should perish, but that all should come to repentance." (II Peter 3:9) So from the earliest days God was looking and watching for any that would respond to His conviction and call and Abram was the first of Joseph's line (Matthew 1:1) and Adam was the first of Mary's line (Luke 3:38) and I believe if we had the full story we would see the 'won by one' precept throughout these generations and at the heart of every conversion is God. How many times have missionaries arrived on a distant shore only to discover that God was there before them? My favorite story on this is when the first missionaries arrived in Japan they already found a Gospel witness. Tracing back the source they discovered that a Gospel tract had washed on shore and from that simple piece of paper the Good News had been spread. In all the excitement of the Great Commission the average Christ has failed to realize: ". . .And **the Lord** added to the church daily such as should be saved." (Acts 2:47) And He still is and still does!

# 2

## WON: SHEM THE SEMITE
## BY: Hebrews 11:7

By faith Noah, being warned of God of things not seen as yet, moved with fear, prepared an ark to the saving of his house; by the which he condemned the world, and became heir of the righteousness which is by faith.

## ONE: NOAH

LIKE WITH ENOCH (GENESIS 5:21-24), Noah was a man who walked with God (Genesis 6:8-9). However, Noah no doubt had many sons that didn't; not until Noah was five hundred years old and Shem was born. I have come to believe that what happened to Enoch at 65 happened to Noah at 500. I have also come to believe that Noah himself never walked with God until he was 500 and that like the other patriarchs before him Moses only recorded those who believed like their fathers. Note, Seth is mentioned for Adam (Genesis 5:3), for we read: "And to Seth, to him also there was born a son; and he called his name Enos: then began men to call upon the name of the LORD." (Genesis 4:26) A study of the genealogy of Jesus in Luke 3:36-38 you will find I believe a list of those who believed and Seth is mentioned after Adam. How many sons and daughters did Adam and Eve have (Genesis 5:4), and though I believe Abel would have been named if he had lived, it was Seth that kept the legacy of his slain brother (Hebrews 11:4). But unlike the others, three sons are mentioned (Genesis 5:32) with Noah and I believe that I could have just as well written on either of them in this 'Won by One' devotional, but for the precept we are trying to underline and highlight I will focus on the oldest, Shem, and how I believe that Noah won him to a saving knowledge of the Almighty God. Shem is important because he maintains the faith link from Adam to Jesus (Luke 3:23–38), a chain I believe that was never broken because of the Biblical precept of 'won by one'!

Why do I believe this action of faith was passed on to Shem? A careful read of Genesis 6:8–10: "But Noah found grace in the eyes of the LORD. These *are* the generations of Noah: Noah was a just man *and* perfect in his generations, *and* Noah walked with God. And Noah begat three sons, Shem, Ham, and Japheth." As I mentioned before, surely in 500 years Noah and Mrs. Noah had other children, but it was Shem, Ham, and Japheth that survived the Flood: "Which sometime were disobedient, when once the longsuffering of God waited in the days of Noah, while the ark was a preparing, wherein few, that is, eight souls (one of those souls was Shem) were saved by water." (I Peter 3:20) Noah was seen as righteous and so was his family of seven at the time of the Flood, for they only entered the ark (Genesis 7:13). What had happened in the 100 years (compare Genesis 5:32 with Genesis 7:11) between the birth of Shem and the going into the ark? I have come to believe that one day Shem was helping build the ark when he was also listening to his father. We often overlook that Noah wasn't just a boat builder, but a preacher as well. Like Enoch before him Noah was warned about the coming 'water judgment' (Genesis 6:13). Noah wasn't just to build a boat (Genesis 6:14–16), but was also commissioned to warn people about it. This truth isn't seen in the Old Testament, but in the New Testament: "And spared not the old world, but saved Noah the eighth *person*, a preacher of righteousness, bringing in the flood upon the world of the ungodly." (II Peter 2:5) We are not told actually how long the ark was being built, but I am persuaded that throughout the time of the building Noah was preaching and one of his converts during that time was his son Shem.

Our key verse printed above tells us that Noah's primary concern was to 'the saving of his house', but I believe as the uniqueness of the ark rising up from the plain drew spectators, and yes, laborers, the uniqueness of the message also drew people. Remember, since creation it hadn't rained: "And every plant of the field before it was in the earth, and every herb of the field before it grew: for the LORD God had not caused it to rain upon the earth, and *there was* not a man to till the ground. But there went up a mist from the earth, and watered the whole face of the ground." (Genesis 2:5–6) Despite the fact most, no all, except his family rejected the message, a wife, three sons and three daughters-in-law eventually believed; believed enough that in the end: "In the selfsame day entered Noah, and Shem, and Ham, and Japheth, the sons of Noah, and Noah's wife, and the three wives of his sons with them, into the ark." (Genesis 7:13) Old enough to marry, strong enough to help with the build, and confounded with his father's message and the pending doom Shem responds. The godly message finally found an entrance into Shem's heart, and when Shem entered the ark he saw it as the only hope for a future!

As we discussed in the first chapter that faith must have action (James 2:17-26), Shem's entrance was that action, but I have come to believe not his only action. I feel Shem's faith is also recognized for his kindness in trying to cover his father's nakedness (Genesis 9:20-21, 23). Unlike Ham, Shem and Japheth tried to restore the dignity of Noah. They had just survived God's divine judgment on a wicked planet and this act showed they wanted 'righteousness' to reign in the new world not the old corruptness. The lust of the eyes and the lust of the flesh (I John 2:16) were inherit in the nature of man and Ham quickly forget that, but Shem hadn't. Like Shem we too must choose not to look (Genesis 9:23), and because Shem and his brother didn't they were blessed (Genesis 9:26-27) while Ham was cursed! (Genesis 9:22, 25) I see Ham as another Lot's wife; a lady that escaped Sodom only to die because her heart was still in Sodom. So with Ham, though he escaped the Flood his heart was still in the old world!

Finally, Shem is recognized as being the ancestor of all Semite people, including the Hebrews. Abram traced his lineage back to Shem (Genesis 11:18-26), and as we have mentioned above that puts Shem in the Messianic Line. Shen was another link in God's chain of redemption. Though we know little else about Shem, he does hold a place of honor in God's divine plan of salvation of the human race, and I have come to believe he is one of the first individuals we can clearly see that fulfills our concept of "won by one". Shem is immortalized in Scripture as a survivor of a divine judgment, an ancestor of the Saviour of the world, and example of what one should do when facing the end of an age. Remember what Jesus taught: "But as the days of Noe *were*, so shall also the coming of the Son of man be. For as in the days that were before the flood' they were eating and drinking, marrying and giving in marriage, until the day that Noe entered into the ark, and knew not until the flood came, and took them all away; so shall also the coming of the Son of man be." (Matthew 24:37-39) We often overlook that the days of Noah were also the days of Shem. Shem put his faith in a ship, but we can put our faith in the Saviour.

Shem I believed helped build the first ark and then he started a race that would produce the second ark in the Person of Jesus Christ. From God's message to Noah to Noah's message to Shem, so too are we not following the same pattern as we share the Gospel given to us by Christ to a family member, a favorite friend and hopefully: won by one!

# 3

## WON: GAIUS THE ROMAN
## BY: III John 1, 4

The elder unto the wellbeloved Gaius, whom I love in the truth.... I have no greater joy than to hear that my children walk in truth.

## ONE: JOHN

Gaius comes from the Latin Caius. We can't be sure of Gaius' race, but I have come to the belief (Romans 14:5) that Gaius was a Roman by birth and through the ministry of the Apostle John became a born-again believer in the Lord Jesus Christ. The reference in our verses printed above to 'my children' was a common phrase of the day connecting a child of God to their earthly spiritual father, or the one that led them to Christ. Paul called Timothy his 'son' (I Timothy 1:2) and Titus his 'son' (Titus 1:4) and Peter called Marcus his 'son' (I Peter 5:13), or child in the faith. I believe John is saying the same of Gaius! We don't have any details of the conversion, but in John's letter to Gaius he was proud that Gaius had grown-up in the 'truth', and in particular the truth about hospitality!

Though Third John is one of the shortest book of the Bible, it does contain three Christian characteristics of the first century church as seem through the three Christians mentioned in the text. When I teach this book, often in connection with the other one chapter books of the Bible, (Obadiah, Philemon, Jude, II John, and II John) I highlight Demetrius for his humility (III John 12), Diotrephes for his haughtiness (III John 9), and Gaius for his hospitality (III John 5–8). When was the last time your local church recognized a church member for their hospitality, and yet

John gives the bulk of this letter to this very topic! This trait, so evident in the first century Church, is sorely lacking in this country, but I have just returned from a land and a Church where hospitality is still an important quality, and Gaius, according to John, was a great example of hospitality.

First, I believe that Gaius teaches the Church that hospitality is INDISCRIMINATE: "Beloved, thou doest faithfully whatsoever thou doest to the brethren, and to strangers." (III John 5) Paul also wrote: "Let brotherly love continue. Be not forgetful to entertain strangers: for thereby some have entertained angels unawares." (Hebrews 13:1–2) Paul also penned: "As we have therefore opportunity, let us do good unto all *men*, especially unto them who are of the household of faith." (Galatians 6:10) An old English saying goes something like this: *"Let the Englishman's castle become the Lord's guest house!"* Do you allow the Lord to use your home to entertain His servants? Gaius received all who came into his house and turned away none, friend or stranger. I believe when people left his home they were the better for it. I have been at it for nearly fifty year and I have made the announcement scores of times of a missionary's visit and who might take them in? Over these decades few have been the volunteers; I rest my case, and I dare say if I was to poll the local pastors the result would be the same, but praise the Lord for the few special people that over the years has practiced such hospitality, and I for one have been made a richer man for being a Gaius (I Timothy 3:2). And I have been blessed, especially in India and Australia, of being treated and helped in my travels in a hospitable way!

Second, I believe that Gaius teaches the Church that hospitality is INTERMEDIATE: "Which have borne witness of thy charity before the church: whom if thou bring forward on their journey after a godly sort, thou shalt do well." (III John 6) Hospitality usually doesn't deal with the beginning or the ending of a journey. Hospitality helps in the middle of a trip. When a man undertakes a work for the Lord the start and the finish are not the toughest parts. There is the excitement of the start, and the relief of the finish, but the middle, the intermediate part has no such joy; that is unless hospitality is shown! Peter tells us: "Use hospitality one to another without grudging." (I Peter 4:9) When missionaries would return home from their mission I believe they would tell of Gaius' hospitality; of how he helped them through the tough and rough times. Like giving (II Corinthians 9:7), hospitality should not be done grudgingly: I have to do it! Have you ever accepted the hospitality of someone and when you got there you felt like a bother? That they were only being hospitable because it was their duty? Not Gaius! People in the middle of their trip need charity not duty. My last trip to India was split up into two, two-week parts. I was greeted in the middle to the home of the Simons of Kerala; a place I had been too five times before and like the previous trips great hospitality was shown.

Third, I believe that Gaius teaches the Church that hospitality is INTRICATE: "Because that for his name's sake they went forth, taking nothing of the Gentiles." (III John 7) I believe that the reason that so much of the work of the Lord is being paid for by unbelievers is the lack of hospitality in the Church. There was a time when the Church of the Living God paid its own way; not asking for handouts from unbelievers! There was a time when the touring evangelist or musician came to the Church and the concert or the meetings were free to the world, but now we have to pay for a hotel because no home is available and the cost isn't paid for by the Church, so an offering has to be taken and some of the money in the plate is from unbelievers. I have watched this trend happen in my lifetime and I have been shocked that we think we need help from the 'Gentiles'. This wasn't true in Gaius' day because of not only hospitality but a belief that the services of the Lord ought to be provided by the servants of the Lord. Could I end this with a story by Richard Halliburton from "The Story of His Life's Adventure": "In 1875, a fleet of Chinese war junks set out to attack California? News had reached the Emperor in Peking that thousands of Chinese who had gone to California to work on the new railroad were being cruelly mistreated, and the outraged Emperor resolved to teach the United States a lesson it wouldn't soon forget. Eastward bound for Monterey sailed seven war junks armed with brass cannon. At least the doughy fleet reached Monterey Bay; 50 gunners stood by the cannon ready to blast the city to pieces if it put up a fight. But far from resisting, the people of Monterey were so delighted with the unexpected visit of Chinese war junks that the whole town can down to the shore to welcome the invaders. The pigtailed warriors, overwhelmed with hospitality, liked California so much that they refused to go home. The older men got jobs on the railroads, and the younger ones stayed on in Monterey as fishermen. The seven junks were ultimately broken up and burned!"

When will we realize that we are 'laborers together with Christ' (I Corinthians 3:9), both in the commission to tell the Gospel to every creature (Mark 16:15), but also after their conversion to help them on their way; whether we provide a place to stay or share with them other teaching of the Christ (Matthew 28:20). Hospitality is not only required in the ministers of the Gospel (Titus 1:8), but in all who minister in the Gospel: "Distributing to the necessity of saints; given to hospitality." (Romans 12:13) One of the aspects that I would like to get across in this series of devotionals I am calling "Won by One' is the precept that once we lead some to the Lord our work is not over, but just beginning. I feel the Church has lost sight of what I call the 'missing link of the commission', and that is help our 'son' or 'daughter' grow: including being hospitable!

# 4

**WON**: THE SAMARITAN WOMAN
**BY**: John 4:29

Come, see a man, which told me all things that ever I did: is not this the Christ?

**ONE**: JESUS

"And He must needs go through Samaria." (John 4:4) Jesus was returning to Galilee by way of Samaria. A map will quickly reveal that Samaria was out of the way, at least there was an easier way back to Jesus' primary field of ministry. Jesus would be considered off track, wasting His time, on a detour earthly speaking, but heavenly speaking Jesus was right on course, right on time, and on the right route. Jesus had an appointment with a woman at a well even through the woman knew nothing about the rendezvous. (John 4:6) Having sent His disciple away to get lunch, and I believe, out of the way, so Jesus was finally alone with this unnamed, but now not unknown woman at Jacob's Well. So began one of the greatest recorded encounters in the Gospels, and certainly a 'won by one' illustration of just how 'one by one' ought to be performed!

The conversation between the Samaritan woman and ultimately the Saviour of that woman began with a simple: "There cometh a woman of Samaria to draw water: Jesus saith unto her, Give me to drink." (John 4:7) A logical and reasonable opening remark to any conversation; talking about what is happening; Jesus was at a well and He was thirsty. Her instant reply: "Then saith the woman of Samaria unto him, How is it that thou, being a Jew, askest drink of me, which am a woman of Samaria? for the Jews have no dealings with the Samaritans." (John 4:9) can be understood with a bit of history. During the days of the Assyrian Captivity (II Kings 17:24), Assyria displaced many of the Jews and replaced them with other races. When the Jews and Gentiles began to inter-marry a new race emerged: Samaritans, named after the region that developed after Israel lost its statehood. Even after the Babylonian Captivity and the Jews began to return a hostility started as seen in Ezra 4:3: "But Zerubbabel, and Jeshua, and the rest of the chief of the fathers of Israel, said unto them, Ye have nothing to do with us to build an house unto our God; but we ourselves together will build unto the LORD God of Israel, as king Cyrus the king of Persia hath commanded us." This hostility only grew with the passing years and by the time of Jesus there was no love lost between the half-Jew, half-Gentile and the Jew because of this precept: "And he said unto them, Ye know how that it is an unlawful thing for a man that is a Jew to keep company, or come unto one of another nation; but God hath shewed me that I should not call any man common or unclean." (Acts 10:28) It was a man-made rule that kept the Samaritans and the Jews separate, but Jesus was determined to correct that concept, for there was a woman to save. Interestingly, when Jesus would give to His disciples the Great Commission, Samaria was second on His priority list (Acts 1:8); his salvation hit-list!

The topic of water, however, soon changed into 'living water' (John 4:10). The woman like Nicodemus was confused at first with this simple explanation of life, especially the reference of "...a well of water springing up into everlasting life..." (John 4:14) Charles Spurgeon, the great English preacher and writer, once made this comment on this transformation: "One in days of yore said, I have been sinking my bucket down into the well full often, but now my thirst after Jesus has become insatiable, that, I long to put the well itself to my lips, and drink right on!" This is what Jesus wanted the woman to do. Forget about the water from the well and drink from the real well: Jesus. Jesus knew this woman as no man before her knew her; He knew what she was really looking for in a man. She had tried six (John 4:17–18), but she needed Jesus. She was trying to quench her thirst in weddings, but it appears that after every affair she was more thirsty. In her sordid relationships and her present adulterous affair, the Samaritan woman was searching for safety, security, and satisfaction in all the wrong places. Later she would say: "Come see a man!" (John 4:29) She finally found the right man in Jesus Christ, but not in a natural relationship, but a spiritual, eternal, satisfying relationship!

Fleece writes: "Because salvation refreshes the soul, the woman at the well because the woman with the well!" All other religions depend on nourishment and refreshments from without, only Christianity can provide both from within. It was this inner spiritual refreshment that Jesus was offering at Jacob's Well. The water was Jesus. From an "Our Daily Bread" devotional I found this: "In the middle ages, people built castles into which they could flee to safety and defend themselves from the enemy. But one of the problems was the water supply. If an enemy surrounded them, they would not have access to life-giving springs and fresh-flowing streams to quench their thirst. Their defeat would be just a matter of time. The problem was solved in the castle of Edinburgh (I visited this castle in Scotland in 2003 with my wife and saw this well), however. It was constructed above an underground spring that gushed forth with all the fresh water the besieged defenders would ever need. Nourished from within, they were practically invulnerable!" That is why Paul encouraged the Corinthians to build their lives over the well (I Corinthians 3:10–11). It is only then we will be able to endure the life-long siege of Satan and Sin that will surround us in this world until we head home for heaven and glory!

As I ponder this idea of Christ as our well, I thought of the different wells that were used on my family homestead in northern Maine. First, there was the well that needed priming. You had to pour water down the well shaft before you could get any water out of it, why? The well kept losing its prime. Nicodemus kept losing his prime (John 3:9, 7:50, 19:39). Each time he had to be provoked before he stood up for the Christ. My grandfather's well had air leaks. Nicodemus had spiritual leaks. The Bible calls them 'grieving the Spirit' (Ephesians 4:30) and 'quenching the Spirit' (I Thessalonians 5:19). Second, there was the deep well by Dad's potato's house. No problem with priming, but it took a lot of pumping. Remember, the woman said the well was deep (John 4:11). The basic problem with the woman at the well is that she was working for her salvation. Despite her sins she was a very religious woman (John 4:20–24). Working might get you water from a deep well, but working will never get you salvation (Ephesians 2:8–9). Third, not far from my home in Perham, Maine was an artesian well. Discovered decades before I was born, it to this very day has been flowing without fail for over a hundred years. I have been to it many times and the flow is crystal clear, sweet water and cold. No priming, no pumping, it just flows. Summer or winter, drought or frost, nothing stops it; much like: ". . .Jesus stood and cried, saying, If any man thirst, let him come unto me, and drink. He that believeth on me, as the scripture hath said, out of his belly shall flow rivers of living water." (John 7:37–38) When the woman at the well believed this she was saved, and she had been lead to that decision because of a conversation with Jesus around a well. Won by one sometimes is as simple as that, and like with the woman it is free (Revelation 22:17). No more priming, no more pumping, just left Him flow through you!

# 5

## WON: TITUS THE GREEK
## BY: Titus 1:4

To Titus, *mine* own son after the common faith: Grace, mercy, *and* peace, from God the Father and the Lord Jesus Christ our Saviour.

## ONE: PAUL

STU WEBER TELLS THIS story under the title of "In the Trenches": "You've probably heard the powerful story coming out of World War One of the deep friendship of two soldiers in the trenches. Two buddies were serving together in the mud and misery of that wretched European stalemate (one version even identifies them as actual brothers). Month after month they lived out their lives in the trenches, in the cold and the mud, under fire and under orders. From time to time one side or the other would rise up out of the trenches, fling their bodies against the opposing line and slink back to lick their wounds, bury their dead, and wait to do it all over again. In the process, friendships were forged in the misery. Two soldiers became particularly close. Day after day, night after night, terror after terror, they talked of life, of families, of hopes, of what they would do when (and if) they returned from this horror. On one fruitless charge, 'Jim' fell, seriously wounded. His friend, 'Bill' made it back to the relative safety of the trenches. Meanwhile Jim lay suffering beneath the night flares. Between the trenches, alone! The shelling continued. The danger was at its peak. Between the trenches was no place to be. Still, Bill wished to reach his friend, to comfort him, to offer encouragement only friends can offer. The officer in charge refused to let Bill leave the trench. It was simply too dangerous. As he turned back, however, Bill went over the top. Ignoring the smell of cordite in the air, the concussion of incoming rounds, and the pounding in his chest, Bill made it to Jim. Sometime later he managed to get Jim back to the safety of the trenches. Too late, his friend was gone. The somewhat self-righteous officer, seeing Jim's body, cynically asked Bill if it had been 'worth' the risk. Bill's response was without hesitation, 'Yes, sir, it was,' he said. 'My friend's last words made it more than worth it. He looked up to me and said, '*I knew you'd come!*'" I believe Paul had such a friend in the spiritual war he and his friend were waging, for we are told on a number of occasions Titus came to Paul: "But neither Titus, who was with me, being a Greek, was compelled to be circumcised." (Galatians 2:3) And from the verse printed above Paul was Titus' son in the faith!

New Testament history of the Church reveals just how true Ecclesiastes 4:9–10 is: "Two *are* better than one; because they have a good reward for their labour. For if they fall, the one will lift up his fellow: but woe to him *that is* alone when he falleth; for *he hath* not another to help him up." When you hear the name of Moody don't you automatically think of Sankey? When you read of Torrey don't you also read of Alexander? When Elijah got so down after the threat of Jezebel didn't God send Elisha (I Kings 19:19–21)? We speak of Moses and Aaron, of Joshua and Caleb, of David and Jonathan, and of Peter and John. If a man, any man finds one true, kindred spirit in his life (women too, Naomi and Ruth come to mind) he has found a pearl of great price. I have come to believe that the Apostle Paul found such a pearl in a Gentile, a Greek named Titus. And what makes this duo so unique is that Paul the Pharisee (Philippians 3:5) wasn't supposed to have any dealing with a man like Titus!

Like with so many of these 'won by one' Bible stories, we don't know exactly when Paul led Titus to Christ, but from the term ology of our key verse printed above, and as we have already see in other chapters this affectionate term of 'mine own son' is the New Testament way of recognizing the fact that it was indeed Paul who was Titus' spiritual father in the Faith. What began in that day was a relationship that would mature into other things as we will see. Every place that Titus is mentioned in the epistles of Paul we see this relationship growing: "Whether *any do enquire* of Titus, *he is* my partner and fellowhelper concerning you: or our brethren *be enquired of, they are* the messengers of the churches, *and* the glory of Christ." (II Corinthians 8:23) There companionship in the ministry is without question and Titus' friendship is clearly seen in verses like II Corinthians 7:6: "Nevertheless God, that comforteth those that are cast down, comforted us by the coming of Titus." I often wonder the more I study the relationship between Paul and Titus if on a number of occasions if Paul didn't say: **"I knew you'd come!"** Titus is first mentioned in a line in Paul's letter to the Corinthians: "I had no rest in my spirit, because I found not Titus my brother: but taking my leave of them, I went from thence into Macedonia." (II Corinthians 2:13) Paul seemingly was dependent on Titus!

Paul and Titus also had the ability to confide in each other: "For if I have boasted any thing to him of you, I am not ashamed; but as we spake all things to you in truth, even so our boasting, which *I made* before Titus, is found a truth." (II Corinthians 7:14) Everybody needs somebody, like Jim and Bill, like Paul and Titus: "Therefore we were comforted in your comfort: yea, and exceedingly the more joyed we for the joy of Titus, because his spirit was refreshed by you all." (II Corinthians 7:13) Paul trusted Titus with important missions: context of our key verse is Paul sending Titus to Crete to set things in order, but we also read this in II Timothy 4:10: "...Titus unto Dalmatia..." But they travelled together as well: "Then fourteen years after I went up again to Jerusalem with Barnabas, and took Titus with *me* also." (Galatians 2:1) Paul and Titus walked in unison and Paul's desire was that others might do the same thing: "I desired Titus, and with *him* I sent a brother. Did Titus make a gain of you? Walked we not in the same spirit? *Walked we* not in the same steps?" (II Corinthians 12:18) Paul and Titus had forged a kinship in Christ that helped each other through the war they were soldiers in.

I feel that what Paul was sharing with us about him and Titus is the classic precept found in Amos 3:3: **"Can two walk together, except they be agreed?"** It of course starts with agreeing on Jesus and after that it can be a struggle as happened with Paul and Barnabas (Acts 15:37-41), but for Paul and Titus that relationship seems to have stayed strong throughout the remainder of Paul's life. "But thanks *be* to God, which put the same earnest care into the heart of Titus for you. For indeed he accepted the exhortation; but being more forward, of his own accord he went unto you. And we have sent with him the brother, whose praise *is* in the gospel throughout all the churches." (II Corinthians 8:16-18) Was Titus Paul's fireman, sent by the Apostle to put our spiritual fires, or a soldier to fight the spiritual battles also raging in the churches? I don't know for sure but no disciple of Paul's is mentioned more in the assignments Paul gave to him as recorded in Paul's epistles than Titus: Crete, Dalmatia, and Corinth!

Do you have a Titus in your life? Do you need a Titus in your life? Again, sooner or later we will all need a Titus, and maybe, just maybe, our Titus is out there but before he or she becomes your Titus you have to lead him or her to a saving knowledge of the Christ. Witnessing can have side benefits we could never imagine!

# 6

## WON: ITTAI THE GITTITE
## BY: II Samuel 15:21

And Ittai answered the king, and said, *As* the LORD liveth, and *as* my lord the king liveth, surely in what place my lord the king shall be, whether in death or life, even there also will thy servant be.

## ONE: DAVID

HUMBOLDT, THE FAMOUS NATURALIST and world traveler, once said that the most wonderful sight he had ever seen was a primrose flourishing on the bosom of a glacier. I have studied David's 'mighty men' (I Chronicles 11:10) for many years and have become fascinated (I have written a devotional book on 105 of them) with the diversity of men that rallied to David's banner. Among my favorites is Ittai, for me, a primrose in David's military garden. What I like most about Ittai is the simple fact when others forsook David during the Absalom Revolt Ittai rose to the occasion and stood by his captain (I Samuel 22:2). Though most of Israel abandoned their King, Ittai took a stand with David and eventually helped David regain the kingship. Ittai proved to be a friend in deed and like the poet once wrote: "The brightest souls which glory ever knew were rocked in storms and nursed when tempest blew!" Why? Because David had led Ittai to his God!

Someone else has written: "It takes hard times to know who your true friends are" and David was facing hard times! When Ittai makes his one and only appearance in the Biblical story, David's kingdom had just been stolen from him by his beloved son Absalom: "And on this manner did Absalom to all Israel that came to the king for judgment: so Absalom stole the hearts of the men of Israel." (II Samuel 15:6) Fearing for the safety of the residents of Jerusalem and the new city David had built on that once Jebusite town, David decided it was best for him to retreat despite the fact that he had made Jerusalem into a nearly impregnable fortress. David's main army was scattered around the borders of the land protecting from an external invasion not realizing an internal revolution was taking place. Instead of resisting Absalom at the gate of Jerusalem, David makes the decision to leave the city to Absalom and gather his army elsewhere! As David prepared to leave the City of David undefended, who should step forward to join him in his ignoble retreat? Not an Israelite, not even a member of his own tribe of Judah, but a Philistine by the name of Ittai. Since boyhood David has been fighting the country of Philistia, the archenemy of Israel. His first direct encounter with a Philistine had been at the Battle of Elah when he faced off against their champion Goliath (I Samuel 17). Who knows, Ittai might have been at that battle? All I know from my study of David's 'mighty men' as the years passed many men from other nations began to join David's Army. I would challenge you to study II Samuel 23 and I Chronicles 11 and 12, the best listings of these special warriors that flocked to David's side over the years before his kingship. I found Ammonites, Hittites, Moabites and Gibeonites serving David, but for me the most startling revelation was the realization that a special detachment of six hundred Gittites, natives of Gath, yes, Goliath's hometown (I Samuel 17:4) were attached to David as seemingly his own personal bodyguard: "And all his servants passed on beside him; and all the Cherethites, and all the Pelethites, and all the Gittites, six hundred men which came after him from Gath, passed on before the king." (II Samuel 15:18) And Ittai was their commander; perhaps, this poem by J. P. McEvery can say best this unique relationship between David and Ittai: "I could sail the waters of the world, bitter and wind and blue, and never I'd find a friend to love, like the friend I've found in you! I could walk down all the roads of the world, and knock on doors forever, and never I'd find a friend like you. Never, never, never!"

Perhaps, it was while David was still fighting King Saul that David meet Ittai, for the Bible tells us that David spend a year and a half in Philistia during the days he was on the run from Saul (I Samuel 27:7). It is my personal opinion (Romans 14:5) that this is when a friendship started with these former adversaries. Ittai was a warrior that was looking for the right cause to fight for and the right leader to follow and he found both in 'the man after God's own heart' (Acts 13:22). During those turbulent years, David was a man without a country and that is why I think David made such an appeal to Ittai before they left Jerusalem: "Then said the king to Ittai the Gittite, Wherefore goest thou also with us? Return to thy place, and abide with the king: for thou *art* a stranger, and also an exile. Whereas thou camest *but* yesterday, should I this day make thee go up and down with us? Seeing I go whither I may, return thou, and take back thy brethren: mercy and truth *be* with thee." (II Samuel 15:19-20) The cause seemed hopeless and the situation dangerous, but Ittai refused to leave David's side: "And Ittai answered the king, and said, *As* the LORD liveth, and *as* my lord the king liveth, surely in what place my lord the king shall be, whether in death or life, even there also will thy servant be." (II Samuel 15:21) This is a man that was brought up to believe in a god that was half man and half fish: Dagon (I Samuel 5)! Ittai's statement to me proves that not only was Ittai a follower of David, but also a follower of David's God. I think what Ittai was saying was the same thing Ruth said to Naomi when her mother-in-law tried to convince her to go home: "And Ruth said, Intreat me not to leave thee, *or* to return from following after thee: for whither thou goest, I will go; and where thou lodgest, I will lodge: thy people *shall be* my people, and thy God my God: where thou diest, will I die, and there will I be buried: the LORD do so to me, and more also, *if ought* but death part thee and me." (Ruth 1:16-17)

I feel W. Glyn Evans express this best in a favorite devotional of mine called "Daily with the King", and I quote: "I must not be satisfied with being a follower of God: I must become a friend of God. Friendship is a polarization of interests, and I must get beyond the point of simply using God as an insurance policy or a life preserver. Friends do not exploit each other, and I must never use my relationship with God as a handy ticket to success or an easy means out of a messy situation!" We forget often that this was the friendship that Jesus promoted among His disciples: "Greater love hath no man than this that a man lay down his life for his ***friends***. Ye are my ***friends***, if ye do whatsoever I command you. Henceforth I call you not servants; for the servant knoweth not what his lord doeth: but I have called you ***friends***; for all things that I have heard of my Father I have made known unto you." (John 15:13-15) It has become my opinion that Ittai had not only switched loyalties, but he had also switched lords. The leaders of the five city-states of Philistia were called lords (Judges 3:3), but now Ittai had a new lord in David and a new Lord in Jehovah.

David not only had the personality and charisma to command such loyalty from his soldiers, but David also believed in a God they could believe in as well and I believe they did. Ittai must have witnessed time after time how God had blessed David, had saved David, had been with David, so eventually Ittai started to believe in David's God: 'won by one' I believe is seen in the relationship David had with this Philistine warrior!

# 7

## WON: DARIUS THE MEDIAN
## BY: Daniel 6:26

I make a decree, That in every dominion of my kingdom men tremble and fear before the God of Daniel: for he *is* the living God, and stedfast for ever, and his kingdom *that* which shall not be destroyed, and his dominion *shall be even* unto the end.

## ONE: DANIEL

I WILL ALWAYS REMEMBER what F. W. Baller wrote concerning his first impression of Hudson Taylor's praying, and I quote: "I had never heard anyone pray like that. There was a simplicity, a tenderness, a boldness, a power that hushed and subdued me, and made it clear that God had admitted him to the inner circle of his friendship!" If we have had the privilege of meeting one great prayer warrior in our lives, they probably changed our lives too. Taylor's prayer sent Baller to China, but I believe Daniel's prayer send Darius to heaven, for that prayer of Daniel's won King Darius to Christ!

Darius the Median was old for that age when he finally accomplished his earthly ambition, the conquest of the Babylonian Empire and their fabled capital at Babylon: "In that night was Belshazzar the king of the Chaldeans slain. And Darius the Median took the kingdom, *being* about threescore and two years old." (Daniel 5:30–31) Darius, with the help of Cyrus the Persian, and governed by God (Proverbs 21:1) established his new kingdom and his new capital in the newly captured city, and there he found a treasure in Daniel: "It pleased Darius to set over the kingdom an hundred and twenty princes, which should be over the whole kingdom; and over these three presidents; of whom Daniel *was* first: that the princes might give accounts unto them, and the king should have no damage. Then this Daniel was preferred above the presidents and princes, because an excellent spirit *was* in him; and the king thought to set him over the whole realm." (Daniel 6:1–3) Darius found an excellent spirit in Daniel; what the kings of Babylon had found also (Daniel 5:12). He found what God already knew: "Though Noah, Daniel, and Job, *were* in it, *as* I live, saith the Lord GOD, they shall deliver neither son nor daughter; they shall *but* deliver their own souls by their righteousness." (Ezekiel 14:20) Oh that we would have such a testimony before God and man; a soul-winning quality as we will see!

Though Daniel was well grounded in his faith, Darius was still gullible. In order to take Daniel out of the race for president, the other contenders plotted Daniel's death. Playing on the pride of Darius (Daniel 6:6) and the devotion of Daniel in prayer (Daniel 6:5), Daniel's enemies crammed through a law that read: ". . .whosoever shall ask a petition of any God or man for thirty days, save of thee, O king, he shall be cast into the den of lion." (Daniel 6:7) Forgetting for a moment Daniel's commitment to pray, Darius signed the bill. Within hours of the law going into effect Daniel was caught praying and was arrested and brought before the king charged with the new offense. "Then the king, when he heard *these* words, **was sore displeased with himself**, and set *his* heart on Daniel to deliver him: and he laboured till the going down of the sun to deliver him." (Daniel 6:14) We can admire Darius' attempt to undo what he had done, but unlike Babylonian law which could be changed by the king, Median law was different: "Now, O king, establish the decree, and sign the writing, that it be not changed, according to the law of the Medes and Persians, which altereth not." (Daniel 6:8) Like with this law, pride and arrogance are qualities that are hard to reverse, and there is only one power strong enough to override such sins, but you have to know that Force before you can change, and though Darius had regrets and he tried to compensate on his own it wasn't enough and never is!

Tried and convicted, Daniel's sentence was carried out by Daniel being thrown into a den of hungry lions. How do I know they were hungry: "And the king commanded, and they brought those men which had accused Daniel, and they cast *them* into the den of lions, them, their children, and their wives; and the lions had the mastery of them, and brake all their bones in pieces or ever they came at the bottom of the den."

(Daniel 6:24) I know you know the rest of the story, but this illustrates what Daniel was facing. But as Daniel was being let down into that lion dungeon, Darius was beginning to see the light; who Daniel was really serving: not the king but God: "Then the king commanded, and they brought Daniel, and cast *him* into the den of lions. *Now* the king spake and said unto Daniel, Thy God whom thou servest continually, he will deliver thee." (Daniel 6:16) Is not this the first step of faith. It was only a mustard seed in size, and it was reflected on another, but it paved the way to a night of fasting and supplication for a friend, but in reality it was the Spirit of God working on a life!

Following that agonizing night, Darius rushes to the den to see if his prayers had been answered: "And when he came to the den, he cried with a lamentable voice unto Daniel: *and* the king spake and said to Daniel, O Daniel, servant of the living God, is thy God, whom thou servest continually, able to deliver thee from the lions?" (Daniel 6:20) They were! It was enough for Darius to make the public decree that we have printed for you at the beginning of this chapter. Is not this Jesus' precept of Matthew 10:32: "Whosoever therefore shall confess me before men, him will I confess also before my Father which is in heaven." I believe that Daniel was the difference in Darius' life. Like with most people before salvation; they must see God in someone else; Darius needed a Daniel and someone might need you to reflect Christ in your life.

I am a preacher of the Gospel today because of those individuals that prayed and lived a consistent witness before me in my youth. We don't know, but I believe Daniel was probably praying for Darius when he was arrested, and we know Daniel was living a godly testimony before Darius. It was the faith of mother Eunice and grandmother Lois that Paul commented (II Timothy 1:5) that resulted in the 'unfeigned faith' of young Timothy (II Timothy 3:15). Paul might have lead Timothy to the Lord (I Timothy 1:18), but it was the prayers and example of Timothy's loved ones that also played a role. Family is one thing, but co-workers can also play a role. It was in the work place that Daniel excelled in soul-winning. Look for other chapters in this book for Daniel's work in other lives! Despite Daniel's tragic deportation to Babylon (Daniel 1), Daniel realized that he still needed to be an example of the believer wherever he was (compare Daniel 1:8 and I Timothy 4:12). As we have already seen in this book God was always looking for souls like Darius (Acts 10:35) in other nations and sometimes God needs to send his ambassadors to those place for people like Darius. Granted, in stories like Darius and

Daniel we have proof, but how many others are not told. I have just returned from a month in India were I saw six ladies come to the saving knowledge of Jesus and like Darius professed their faith in him. If I had never gone would they have been saved? God has chosen soles for souls. Remember the old question: Would there be enough evidence to convict you of being a Christian if you were arrested?" Think about it, for I believe a soul may depend on your answer. I believe this was the case with Darius and Daniel!

# 8

## WON: THE ETHIOPIAN EUNUCH
## BY: Acts 8:37

And Philip said, If thou believest with all thine heart, thou mayest. And he answered and said, I believe that Jesus Christ is the Son of God.

## ONE: PHILIP

WHO HAS NOT HEARD of this unnamed but not unknown eunuch from Ethiopia? I believe this amazing conversion was recorded in the Book of Acts to underline and highlight the importance of the great doctrine of baptism; a much defined and misused sacrament of the Church, yet one that has stood the test of time, and has come forth triumphantly. But before baptism can take place salvation must be in place and Philip and the eunuch are a wonderful illustration of making sure you get the horse before the cart!

The story doesn't begin with baptism, but salvation; so too the relationship with baptism. Years ago I baptized a lady that had been baptized as a child, despite the fact she hadn't yet been converted. Though salvation is the theme of this story, baptism is the topic. It is the initial rite following salvation. It is the outward ritual that publicly confirms an individual's private conversion to Christianity! Jesus commanded it just before he returned to the Father: "Go ye therefore, and teach all nations, baptizing them in the name of the Father, and of the Son, and of the Holy Ghost." (Matthew 28:19) About three thousand were baptized at Pentecost following their conversion (Acts 2:38). The Samaritans were baptized following the great revival that sweep through their country (Acts 8:12).

It was during that great revival that Philip was called away to meet the eunuch. Paul the great persecutor of the Church was baptized following his dramatic conversion on the road to Damascus (Acts 9:18). Paul would make it an important part of his ministry (Acts 22:16), as have I. I have just returned from a mission's trip to India where I had the privilege of participating in 14 young people getting baptized! Cornelius the centurion (Acts 10:47–48), Lydia, a seller of purple garments (Acts 16:15), and the Philippian jailer and his family (Acts 16:33) all were baptized, and the moment the Ethiopian eunuch believed he asked to be baptized: "And as they went on *their* way, they came unto a certain water: and the eunuch said, See, *here is* water; what doth hinder me to be baptized?" (Acts 8:36) Baptism is a very important part of our salvation. Baptism doesn't save us, but it is the first sign that salvation has come to a believer!

This famous eunuch, or castrated man, was the treasurer of the Queen of Ethiopia. Candace was a title given to the Queen of Nubia, a country on the Nile near the vicinity of Khartoum (Acts 8:27). Interestingly, under Mosaic law a eunuch was placed under serious religious restrictions. Though the eunuch could worship in Jerusalem, he was not allowed to enter the Temple in Jerusalem (Deuteronomy 23:1). Perhaps, that is what this eunuch was looking for that day he was setting quietly in his chariot in Gaza? Rejected by the Jewish faith, he was seeking another as he studied the Old Testament prophet Isaiah. I feel the eunuch's conversion demonstrates the outreach Christianity should have to all the races, all the religions, and all the restricted people groups in the world. Christ's Gospel embraces all, the whole, the half, the disabled, and the deformed. The eunuch left Jerusalem lacking something for which his soul was still craving, still searching; a proselyte (one who has switched religions) for sure, but not yet a product of a faith saving experience. A non-Jew that was looking for God outside his own land, and it was not until he had gone through Judea and Jerusalem that he found Jesus on a lonely desert road in Gaza. I know not what you must go through to get to Jesus, but if you search and find Him, who alone can save, your search will stop with Him! "Then Philip opened his mouth, and began at the same scripture, and preached unto him Jesus." (Acts 8:35)

The only way the Ethiopian Eunuch could have known about baptism is if Philip had mentioned it during their conversation. Baptism was not a Jewish ritual, or an Ethiopian rite. Baptism was first connected with John the Baptist, and adapted by Jesus into His Church. Maybe Philip repeated the words of Peter when he was asked after his great message on

Pentecost: "Now when they heard *this*, they were pricked in their heart, and said unto Peter and to the rest of the apostles, Men *and* brethren, what shall we do? Then Peter said unto them, Repent, and be baptized every one of you in the name of Jesus Christ for the remission of sins, and ye shall receive the gift of the Holy Ghost." (Acts 2:37-38) The eunuch's question about baptism (Acts 8:36) was followed by a profession of faith (Acts 8:37) which was enough for Philip to baptize the Ethiopian Eunuch (Acts 8:38)! Charles Spurgeon writing in his classic devotional "Morning and Evening" says this about the eunuch's testifying about the Christ, and I quote: "These words may answer your scruples, devout reader, concerning the ordinances. Perhaps you say, 'I should be afraid to be baptized; it is such a solemn thing to avow myself to be dead with Christ, and buried with Him.' (Romans 6:1-4) Ah! Poor trembler, Jesus has given you liberty, be not afraid. When the Holy Spirit has given you to feel the spirit of adoption, you may come to Christians ordinances without fear. The same rule holds good of the Christian's inward privileges. You think, poor seeker, that you are not allowed to rejoice with joy unspeakable (I Peter 1:8) and full glory; if you are permitted to get inside Christ's door, or sit at the bottom of His table, you will be content. Ah! But you shall not have less privileges than the very greatest. God makes no difference in His love to His children. A child is a child to Him; He will not make him a hired servant; but he shall feast upon the fatted calf (Luke 15:29-23), and shall have music and dancing as much as if he had never gone astray. When Jesus comes into the heart, he issues a general license to be glad in the Lord. No chains are worn in the court of King Jesus. Our admission into full privileges may be gradual, but it is sure!" I feel this is what the Ethiopian eunuch felt that day and that is why he was bold with Philip in asking about baptism.

Dear friend, have you like the eunuch been to the waters yet? Have you like him "...come up out of the water?" (Acts 8:39) The grace that Christ offers now overcomes all racial barriers. It grants you no matter your color or former creed a full and complete acceptance into the family of God (Galatians 3:26) immediately. If this be true and I believe it is, then why not share your new found faith by a public demonstration before family and friends through baptism! The immersing waters will be your public coming out party of your profession of faith in the death, burial, and resurrection of Jesus Christ. Though of an honorable position and place, this eunuch had been shunned by the exclusive Law of Moses, yet in Jesus he found grace and truth (John 1:17), and this is why when his experience with Philip was over ". . .he went on his way rejoicing!" (Acts 8:39) Until you are baptized you will not have the full joy that is yours in Jesus Christ because you have not obeyed one of His laws (Mark 16:16). For you see, baptism isn't a choice, but a commandment. Philip is the one that won the Ethiopian eunuch to the Lord, but he is also the one that lead him into the waters of baptism as a testimony of that faith.

# 9

## WON: ELIEZER THE SYRIAN
## BY: Genesis 24:12

And he said, O LORD God of my master Abraham, I pray thee, send me good speed this day, and shew kindness unto my master Abraham.

## ONE: ABRAHAM

Eliezer is only mentioned once by name in the Scriptures, but his contribution to the textual story is invaluable in our journey through the 'won by one' illustrations in the Bible: "After these things the word of the LORD came unto Abram in a vision, saying, Fear not, Abram: I *am* thy shield, *and* thy exceeding great reward. And Abram said, Lord GOD, what wilt thou give me, seeing I go childless, and the steward of my house *is* this Eliezer of Damascus?" (Genesis 15:1-2) Abraham had a man to witness too!

Where Abraham picked up Eliezer we are not told, but no doubt during his trip from Haran to Canaan; Damascus, the capital of Syria, would be on the way. (Genesis 12:5) When Eliezer started to believe in Abraham's God is also not mentioned. It is my belief that as Abraham grew in faith, he shared that faith with the people of his household. Remember, Abram was first an idol worshipper (Joshua 24:2), but when the Lord God appeared to him things changed: "By faith Abraham, when he was called to go out into a place which he should after receive for an inheritance, obeyed; and he went out, not knowing whither he went." (Hebrews 11:8) All I know about Eliezer is that by the time he is sent by Abraham back to Haran to get a bride for Isaac he is showing all the signs of a true believer in Jehovah. I would show you these signs of salvation by his faith in finding the right wife for his master's son.

With the divorce rate now fifty percent, and with the Christian trend following the world's example, I think it is about time we take seriously the example of 'Damascus Eliezer'! Who you would ask? Is he some new revolutionary marriage counsellor, or maybe, a new family psychologist with a radical new philosophy on marriage? None of the above! He was Abraham's chief servant that was given what most would say was an impossible task: finding a wife for another man. The only knowledge I have of this is my experiences in India where this practice is still happening. I know I wouldn't want to do it, and I am glad I picked my own wife, but I did apply Eliezer's techniques to my selection, and I have been advising would-be brides and bridegroom for fifty years to follow Eliezer's practices. If you are getting ready to get married or you know someone who is I think it would be wise for you to tell them to read the story of Genesis 24. It is one of those rare Genesis stories that is given an entire chapter, for me making it important, and besides, it is one of the longest chapters in Genesis: sixty-seven verses. I would refer you to Dr. Damascus Eliezer, the Syrian believer who learned to trust God with life's most difficult and important questions. I have preached for decades that the three most important questions are: what you will do with the Christ? Who you will marry, and what will you do with your life?

Eliezer's one call to Biblical fame is the story of how Isaac found Rebekah. Abraham's Sarah had died (Genesis 25:23), and I feel that Abraham through his life was running out (Abraham was 137 at Sarah's departure, but he would live to 175-Genesis 25:7, but he didn't know that). There was one thing he had to do and that was to find a wife for Isaac (Isaac would have been 37 at his mother's death-Genesis 21:5). His instructions were clear: no bride from Canaan (Genesis 24:3-4), but a wife from his family back in Haran. In the end Eliezer agreed to follow his master's directions and return to Haran to find the wife Abraham wanted for Isaac. (Genesis 24:9) So off Eliezer went and as he neared the city of Nahor, he realized the seriousness of his task and sought help, but from whom? A match maker in Nahor? No! Eliezer applied James 1:5, you know if any man lack wisdom. Read again the verse we have printed at the top of this chapter! I believe as Abraham was praying in Canaan Eliezer was praying in Nahor. No marriage should be joined until every party involved in a marriage saturates the union on prayerful consideration. From the pen of Paul we have: "Be careful for nothing; but in everything (including marriage) by prayer and supplication with thanksgiving let your requests be made known unto God." (Philippians 4:6) But how many pray about this second most important choice of your life? Pray now or pay later ought to be the motto of all seeking a mate for marriage. But for me, in this article this is the first sign that Eliezer was not trusting in another god, but in Abraham's God, for salvation and for service!

The second precept that came to me was found in Genesis 24:14: "And let it come to pass, that the damsel to whom I shall say, Let down thy pitcher, I pray thee, that I may drink; and she shall say, Drink, and I will give thy camels drink also: *let the same be* she *that* thou hast appointed for thy servant Isaac; and thereby shall I know that thou hast shewed kindness unto my master." Eliezer was seeking God's choice, not Abraham's choice, nor Eliezer's choice. Another wonderful sign of conversion: 'Thy will be done!' Later Jacob's choice was Rachel (Jacob still in the flesh), but God's choice was Leah (Genesis 49:31-even Jacob would recognize this in the end), for it was through Leah the Messianic Line would come (Genesis 29:35). Who is God looking for: "While they behold your chaste conversation *coupled* with fear. Whose adorning let it not be that outward *adorning* of plaiting the hair, and of wearing of gold, or of putting on of apparel; but *let it be* the hidden man of the heart, in that which is not corruptible, *even the ornament* of a meek and quiet spirit, which is in the sight of God of great price." (I Peter 3:2–4) And we know that God's choice became Isaac's choice (Genesis 24:67), but for our purpose we see again Eliezer living an example seen in Scripture "as being the example of a believer". (I Timothy 4:12)

What has always been a highlight in this story is Genesis 24:15: "And it came to pass, **before he had done speaking**, that, behold, Rebekah came out, who was born to Bethuel, son of Milcah, the wife of Nahor, Abraham's brother, with her pitcher upon her shoulder." Another sign of salvation is when the Good Lord honors His child's request. Even before Eliezer finished praying the answer was on the way. I always liken this to what happened when Peter was preaching to Cornelius and his household: "**While Peter yet spake these words**, the Holy Ghost fell on all them which heard the word." (Acts 10:44) In other words before the evangelist had finished his invitation the sinners listening to him were already saved. The Holy Ghost would have never fallen if salvation hadn't taken place in the heart. And so it was with Eliezer as he demonstrated his trust in Jehovah and in Jehovah alone. Read the rest of the story and you will see again and again Eliezer giving credit to God for all that took place. Isn't this a sign of a believer?

The final verse I would like for you to see is Genesis 24:48: "And I bowed down my head, and worshipped the LORD, and blessed the LORD God of my master Abraham, which had led me in the right way to take my master's brother's daughter unto his son."

# 10

## WON: BARTIMAEUS THE BLINDMAN
## BY: Mark 10:52

And Jesus said unto him, Go thy way; thy faith hath made thee whole. And immediately he received his sight, and followed Jesus in the way.

## ONE: JESUS

SOLOMON WROTE CENTURIES BEFORE Jesus meet Bartimaeus: "To every-thing *there is* a season, and a time to every purpose under the heaven. . .a time to keep silence, and a time to speak." (Ecclesiastes 3:1, 7) If there is anything I like it is silence, quietness, but if there is anything I hate it is silence when you ought to be shouting, screaming! For our 'WON BY ONE' character for this article I have reminded you above of an encounter when Jesus was passing by a Blindman outside the city of Jericho, and for Bartimaeus it wasn't a time to remain silent, but a time to shout: "And when he heard that it was Jesus of Nazareth, he **began to cry out**, and say, Jesus, *thou* Son of David, have mercy on me. And many charged him that he should hold his peace (keep silent): but he cried the more a great deal, *Thou* Son of David, have mercy on me." (Mark 10:47-48) This Blindman was ready to scream, cry out, shout out for he wanted to get Jesus attention; Bartimaeus was in need, so why wouldn't he yell? Despite the crowd's rebuke, sneers, and criticism he cried even more, got even louder. I believe Bartimaeus has a lesson for us to learn in the way he carried himself that day outside Jericho, for he was not just seeking a healing!

There is a time to be silent, and there is a time to shout and make sure everybody knows what side you are on. In the story of Bartimaeus we are challenged because for too long most sinners have been silent for far too long. For far too long the Church and Christians have been silent when we should have been speaking as Paul exhorts: "But if our gospel be hid, it is hid to them that are lost." (II Corinthians 4:3) And for far too long we have been shouting when we should have been silent as James exhorts: "Wherefore, my beloved brethren, let every man be swift to hear, slow to speak, slow to wrath." (James 1:19) There is a holy balance here that can only be applied in the spiritual realm by the Spirit of God in our lives; when to be silent and when to speak. The case for Bartimaeus was clear, for him it was a time to shout. On the other hand there are times when 'slow to speak' is the important factor in the situation or circumstance you find yourself in, but for this devotional I am highlighting and underlining the latter!

The Church of God today has seemingly missed this key teaching of Jesus: "Whosoever therefore shall confess me before men, him will I confess also before my Father which is in heaven. But whosoever shall deny me before men, him will I also deny before my Father which is in heaven." (Matthew 10:32–33) I am afraid there are too many Christians setting in the pew bleachers of a church and nobody knows really what side they are on. I have always made it clear in my teaching and preaching where I stand, on whose side I am on, and often the people around the meeting hear me as clearly as those in the meeting. I wondered for a while why God gave me a big voice; I am loud when I whisper. My wife was always (she passed into Glory in 2020) tugging on my shirt to quiet down when I was in just a casual conversation with someone. I tell people that in my nursing home services I am preaching to the deaf in the congregation as well as the cook in the kitchen down the hall! Like at a baseball game some say pipe down, tone it down, keep it down, but I say that is just the beginning of shutting it down! That is why I love the Bartimaeus story. He was just an ordinary blind beggar beside a road with no hope and helpless to help himself. Then one day in his silence he heard a ray of hope. Bartimaeus didn't know that Jesus had come to heal him, just like the time Jesus came to Jericho to save Zacchaeus (Luke 19:1–10), or the Samarian woman knew that Jesus was passing though Samaria just for her (John 4:4)! But Bartimaeus wasn't going to take any chances that Jesus would miss him, for he began to yell, shout out. Granted, Bartimaeus made a fool of himself beside the Jericho Road, but he didn't care because he was looking for mercy (Mark 10:48)!

And because of all that shouting the rest of the story is clear: "And Jesus stood still, and commanded him to be called. And they call the blind man, saying unto him, be of good comfort, rise; he calleth thee. And he, casting away his garment, rose, and came to Jesus. And Jesus answered and said unto him, what wilt thou that I should do unto thee? The blind man said unto him, Lord, that I might receive my sight. And Jesus said unto him, Go thy way; thy faith hath made thee whole. And immediately he received his sight, and followed Jesus in the way." (Mark 10:49-52) What is clear to me is that day Bartimaeus was not only physically headed but spiritually healed as well. It started with his recognition that Jesus was the "Son of David' a Messianic title, so Bartimaeus believed that Jesus had come to save him, and not just his sight (Isaiah 61:1-2). And he believed what Paul would later write: "For the scripture saith, Whosoever believeth on him shall not be ashamed (he wasn't on that road side outside of Jericho). For there is no difference between the Jew and the Greek: for the same Lord over all is rich unto all that call upon him. For whosoever shall call (Bartimaeus certainly called) upon the name of the Lord shall be saved." (Romans 10:11-13) And what did Jesus say: "Thy faith"! Did not Bartimaeus fulfill the instructions of Romans 10:9-10: "That if thou shalt confess with thy mouth the Lord Jesus, and shalt believe in thine heart that God hath raised him from the dead, thou shalt be saved. For with the heart man believeth unto righteousness; and with the mouth confession is made unto salvation."

Are you today blinded by Satan (II Corinthians 4:4)? This is not the day of silence but of shouting out for the Lord's help. Remember the cry of the Philippian jailer: "And brought them out, and said, Sirs, what must I do to be saved?" (Acts 16:30) Warning, like Bartimaeus, you too might be confronted by a friend or even a parent that might try to keep you silent, that this is not the best time, keep still, don't act like a fool. My advice is to cry out because "Seek ye the Lord while he may be found, call ye upon him while he is near." (Isaiah 55:6) It wouldn't have done Bartimaeus any good to wait until Jesus was in Jerusalem. Jesus was near and the Blindman started to shout. Paul also warns the Corinthian Church: "(For he saith, I have heard thee in a time accepted, and in the day of salvation have I succoured thee: behold, now *is* the accepted time; behold, now *is* the day of salvation.)" (II Corinthians 6:2) If Bartimaeus would have waited till the next day to shout he would have missed Jesus; just like many miss the Saviour because they miss the 'time', 'the day of salvation' which is now! This is not the time to be silent, this is not the time to be still; this is the time for action, calling, yes, shouting, yelling "...have mercy on me!" Whether I am speaking to a saint or a sinner in this article I hope you have gotten the point of this challenge. Dear unsaved friend please speak up and asked the dear Saviour to save you today, tomorrow might be too late. Dear saint please take very opportunity to speak up for Jesus because it is important that people know where you stand and who you believe, because this is no time to be hiding the Gospel of Jesus!

# 11

## WON: EBEDMELECH THE ETHIOPIAN
## BY: Jeremiah 39:18

For I will surely deliver thee, and thou shalt not fall by the sword, but thy life shall be for a prey unto thee: because thou hast put thy trust in me, saith the LORD.

## ONE: JEREMIAH

ONE OF THE UNSUNG heroes of the Old Testament has to be Ebedmelech, the Ethiopian: "Now when Ebedmelech the Ethiopian, one of the eunuchs which was in the king's house, heard that they had put Jeremiah in the dungeon; the king then sitting in the gate of Benjamin." (Jeremiah 38:7) A servant of King Zedekiah of Judah, it was Ebedmelech who interceded for the prophet Jeremiah and eventually saved his life: "Ebedmelech went forth out of the king's house, and spake to the king, saying, My lord the king, these men have done evil in all that they have done to Jeremiah the prophet, whom they have cast into the dungeon; and he is like to die for hunger in the place where he is: for *there is* no more bread in the city." (Jeremiah 34:8-9) With the king's permission, Ebedmelech lowered a rope into a miry pit that Jeremiah had been put in because he was preaching that the Jews should surrender to the Babylonians. Ebedmelech hauled the nearly dead prophet out of his dungeon allowing Jeremiah to return to his prophecies (Jeremiah 34:10-13), but I believe the relationship between the Ethiopian and the Jew also resulted in another glorious illustration of 'won by one'!

The first result of Jeremiah's rescue was a promise to Ebedmelech that in the up and coming occupation of Jerusalem by the Babylonians that Ebedmelech would not be killed: "Now the word of the LORD came unto Jeremiah, while he was shut up in the court of the prison, saying, go and speak to Ebedmelech the Ethiopian, saying, Thus saith the LORD of hosts, the God of Israel; Behold, I will bring my words upon this city for evil, and not for good; and they shall be *accomplished* in that day before thee. But I will deliver thee in that day, saith the LORD: and thou shalt not be given into the hand of the men of whom thou *art* afraid." (Jeremiah 39:15–17) So what was it about this foreigner that stood out to God, fulfilling again Peter's conclusion: "But in every nation he that feareth him, and worketh righteousness, is accepted with him" (Acts 10:35)? What was it about Jeremiah that caused this stranger to help the unpopular prophet when Jeremiah's own country-men wouldn't lift a finger to help him? So what was the relationship between Jeremiah and Ebedmelech that resulted in the conversion of this man?

I feel the answer to all these questions can be summarized in one word: trust, and trust is the key to salvation whether the Old Testament times, the New Testament times, or our times. In God's explanation to Jeremiah why Ebedmelech would be spared during the Babylonian Captivity He said this: "For I will surely deliver thee, and thou shalt not fall by the sword, but thy life shall be for a prey unto thee: **because thou hast put thy trust in me**, saith the LORD." (Jeremiah 39:18) Trusting in God allows you to do things that others won't even attempt. It was trust in God that he was doing right when he approached Zedekiah to save Jeremiah's life when all the rest of Zedekiah's counselors where speaking of Jeremiah's execution because he was a traitor. (Jeremiah 38:9) It was trust in Jeremiah's God that allowed Ebedmelech to convince the king to let Jeremiah go: "Then the king commanded Ebedmelech the Ethiopian, saying, Take from hence thirty men with thee, and take up Jeremiah the prophet out of the dungeon, before he die." (Jeremiah 38:10) And I believe that it was trust in God that motivated Ebedmelech's heart to be compassionate and concerned about the man of God (Jeremiah 38:11–12) Centuries later Jesus would quote Isaiah in these words: **"And in his name shall the Gentiles trust."** (Matthew 12:21) We overlook the fact that despite the fact that the Bible is mostly a Jewish book, many outside the Jewish race also put there trust in Jehovah God. We are going to see many of them in this book, for Ebedmelech was just one. Paul would make this observation in Romans: "And again, Esaias saith, There shall be a root of Jesse, and he that shall rise to reign over the Gentiles; *in him shall the Gentiles trust."* (Romans 15:12) And Ebedmelech was one of those Gentiles!

David the psalmist would write: "...Blessed *are* all they that put their trust in him." (Psalm 2:12) I believe Ebedmelech's act of trust saved his life and the life of the prophet. Today, the action is the same, by putting your trust in the Lord Jesus Christ you too will be saved. Oswald Chambers wrote this about trust in his famous devotional book "My Utmost for His Highest", and I quote: "Put God first in trust. Our Lord trusted no man (John 2:24–25); yet He was man, because He put God first in His trust; He trusted absolutely in what God's grace could do for any man. If I put my trust in human beings first, I will end in despairing of everyone; I will become bitter, because I have insisted on man being what no man ever can be-absolutely right. Never trust anything but the grace of God in yourself or in anyone else!" I have come to believe (Romans 14:5) that this was the kind of trust Ebedmelech developed as he listened to the prophet of God; he was trusting in God but where did he learn to trust; who taught him about trust. I am convinced that through the years of watching and listening to Jeremiah, while the Jews rejected his example and message, Ebedmelech was learning to believe in trust, so God was using 'the weeping prophet' to direct Ebedmelech unto Himself.

Ebedmelech was just a forerunner of the more famous Ethiopian eunuch who put his trust in Jesus through the testimony and teaching of Philip immortalized through the pen of Luke in Acts 8. Who knows if the faith of Ebedmelech had not been passed down through time. Why was the Ethiopian eunuch traveling to Jerualem in the first place? It seems that the Ethiopian eunuch was already a proselyte (Acts 2:9), so where did the Ethiopians learn about Jehovah? Did Ebedmelech return to his country after his release by the Babylonians and share the truth about the True and Living God? We don't have any answers to these questions, for our unsung hero leaves the sacred Word just as quickly as he appears. Six times (Jeremiah 38:7, 8, 10, 11, 12, 39:12) Ebedmelech's name appears in just two chapters and all around his rescue of Jeremiah. But as for me, I can't but believe that the trust he showed and the actions he did are not the essential instruction of James: "Even so faith, if it hath not works, is dead, being alone. Yea, a man may say, Thou hast faith, and I have works: shew me thy faith without thy works, and I will shew thee my faith by my works." (James 2:17–18) Ebedmelech had both and demonstrated both, so such faith and works will reproduce itself in others and though the two Ethiopian stories are hundreds of year apart they still contain the same elements important for salvation. Jeremiah didn't find many that would put their faith in his Gospel, but he found Ebedmelech and who knows if Ebedmelech didn't become Ebedmelech the evangelist setting the stage for Philip's eunuch? When I think of Jeremiah I think of this precept: "They that sow in tears shall reap in joy." (Psalm 126:5) Jeremiah sowed in tears and reaped in the person of an Ethiopian by the name of Ebedmelech!

# 12

## WON: THE PHILIPPIAN JAILER
## BY: Acts 16:34

And when he had brought them into his house, he set meat before them, and rejoiced, believing in God with all his house.

## ONE: PAUL

IN MY OPINION, ONE of the greatest salvation stories recorded in the Bible has to do with the conversion of the Philippian jailer and his family. Most know the story well: as Paul and Silas prayed and sang at midnight (Acts 16:25), the Almighty God opened the prison doors at Philippi with a mighty earthquake (Acts 16:26). What was Paul praying for? In a lifetime of study of the person of Paul, I have come to the conclusion that the character of Paul wouldn't make me believe he was praying for a release from his jail cell, but for the soul of the jailer (Acts 16:27), and now we know the souls of the jailer's family. Had Paul and the jailer had a conversation or two, for why else would the jailer ask what I believe to be the world's most famous, and important question? (Acts 16:30) Note how personal the question was, but notice how far reaching the answer was: "And they said, Believe on the Lord Jesus Christ, and thou shalt be saved, *and thy house.*" (Acts 16:31) Also notice 'they said', for we often ignore Silas in this story. I know this book is 'Won by One' but we might have to say here: won by two!

I was challenged recently by this devotional from the pen of Charles H. Spurgeon from his classic book "Morning and Evening", and I quote: "This gospel from a man with a sword at his throat is the gospel for me.

This would suit me if I were dying, and it is all that I need while I am living. I took away from self and sin and all idea of personal merit, and I trust the Lord Jesus as the Saviour whom God has given. I believe in Him; I rest in Him; I accept Him to be my all in all. Lord I am save, and I shall be saved to all eternity, for I believe in Jesus. Blessed be Thy name for this. May I daily prove by my life that I am saved from selfishness and worldliness and from every form of evil, but those last words about my 'house', Lord? I would not run away with half a promise when thou doest give a whole one. I beseech Thee, save all my family. Save the nearest and dearest. Convert the children, and the grandchildren, if I have any. Be gracious to my servants and all who dwell under my roof or work with me. Thou makest this promise to me personally if I believe in the Lord Jesus. I beseech Thee to do thou hast said. I would go over in my prayer every day the names of all my brothers and sisters, parents, children, friends, relatives, and servants, and give Thee no rest till that word is fulfilled: 'and thy house'!" In our focus on the conversion of the jailer we forget that he wasn't the only person that got saved that day: "And they spake unto him the word of the Lord, and to all that were in his house. And he took them the same hour of the night, and washed *their* stripes; and was baptized, he and all his, straightway." (Acts 16:32–33) Amen and Amen!

The reason this simple devotional touched my heart was at the time I was concerned about a member of my family. A cherished son who made a profession of faith as a young boy is now not living that confession. I was encouraged by Spurgeon's words and I was challenged again to look at this familiar story of the Jailer, and this is what blessed me. A Christian hymn called "A Christian Home" written by Barbara B. Hart contains these words: "O give us homes built firm upon the Saviour, where Christ is Head and Counsellor and Guide; where every child is taught His love and favor, and gives his heart to Christ the crucified. . .O give us homes with godly fathers, mothers, who always place their hope and trust in Him; whose tender patience turmoil never bothers. . .a home where each finds joy in serving other. . .O Lord, our God, our homes are Thine forever. . ." Rare are those homes today (postscript-before my son Scott died at 39 from cancer He did return fulfilling another promise: "Train up a child in the way he should go: and when he is old, he will not depart from it." Proverbs 22:6), but what an example can be found in this Philippian home of the unnamed jailer of Philippi. I gleaned this:

1. A HOME THAT BELIEVED TOGETHER. Can a home really be a home unless the family is one in Christ? Oh, I know you can give the title of family to any combination of individuals as we are doing today, but a true family is a unified family under the belief of what Jesus did for each member of that family at Calvary. One of the problems with families today is they are not saved, or the family is split: saved and unsaved (Amos 3:3), and until all are saved there will be fractures and frustrations and fights within the family circle.

2. A HOME BANDED TOGETHER. We are not given many detail, but after the jailer's encounter with Paul and Silas in the jail he was determined to take the pair home. This is not rare in the conversions stories of the Bible; a desire that other might know and especially those others being family and friends. Remember what the tax collector Matthew did after he met Jesus? Remember he invited his friends to a party, and though we are not total probably his family (Matthew 9:9-10). A believer's first missionfield is to his own family, (Luke 8:39) and when the jailer's family heard the Good News from the lips of Paul they too got saved!

3. A HOME THAT WAS BAPTIZED TOGETHER. One of the great honors and privileges of being a pastor is baptism. As I rewrite this chapter I have just returned from the State of Chhattisgarh in India where one of the blessings was to baptize fourteen. Seven of the fourteen were from the Nag family; not one family but a group of related families. I baptized two brothers and two sister from the Kashyap family. Over the years I have baptized all kinds of combinations like a mother and her three sons, fathers and mothers and their children, and so many more in my now 49 baptisms. The jailer's family got saved together and they got baptized together, a memory unforgotten. I was baptized with my older sister in 1964, and had the thrill of baptizing my son and daughter at the same time!

4. A HOME THAT WAS BLESSED TOGETHER. "And when he had brought them into his house, he set meat before them, and rejoiced, believing in God with all his house." (Acts 16:34) Remember what the shepherd did when he found his lost sheep? (Luke 15:6) Remember what the woman did when she found her lost silver coin? (Luke 15:9) Remember what the father did when his prodigal son returned home? (Luke 15:23) Why would we be surprised that there was a party, a rejoicing, at the Philippian Jailer's House? Remember

Jesus taught in his famous 'lost parables': "Likewise, I say unto you, there is joy in the presence of the angels of God over one sinner that repenteth." (Luke 15:10) If the angels rejoice over one, what do they do over an entire family?

This wouldn't be the only recorded family conversion in the Bible: "And Crispus, the chief ruler of the synagogue, believed on the Lord with all his house; and many of the Corinthians hearing believed, and were baptized." (Acts 18:8) In Paul's desire to win one, he also saw beyond the one to the ones behind the one, and so should we!

# 13

## WON: MARCUS THE JEW
## BY: I Peter 5:13

The *church that is* at Babylon, elected together with *you*, saluteth you; and *so doth* Marcus my son.

## ONE: PETER

JOHN MARK IS AN often overlooked, but I believe an important biographical study in the Bible. His scriptural story is an example that many believers emulate: the roller coaster pilgrimage I call it. Most believer find in time that their Christianity has many ups and downs, curves and dips, and twists and turns galore. Marcus was raised in a godly home, and at a very young age witnessed some of the great events of the early Church: "And when he had considered *the thing*, he came to the house of Mary the mother of **John, whose surname was Mark**; where many were gathered together praying." (Acts 12:12) I believe Mark was there the night Peter escaped his death sentence and appeared unexpectedly at his family's door. For me, this is one of the events that links Peter to Marcus and the verse printed above where Peter recognizes Marcus as his spiritual son!

I am convinced as are many others that John Mark was in the Garden of Gethsemane the night that Jesus was arrested: And there followed him a certain young man, having a linen cloth cast about *his* naked *body*; and the young men laid hold on him: and he left the linen cloth, and fled from them naked." (Mark 14:51–52) Only the author of the Gospel according to Mark would have known this detail which also makes me believe that the home that Peter escaped too years later was the same home that the famous Last Supper was shared. It is my believe that the man of the house that lead the two disciples there to prepare the Passover was Mark's father and we know that his mother Mary was a follower of the Christ. I feel Mark was just a boy and as boys would do despite probably being sent to bed he was curious enough to follow Jesus and his disciples to the garden where he was found out. From my study of Mark's life he appears to be the adventures type, so the escape from Gethsemane naked fits the profile of the future missionary. There are even some like myself that believe Mark's Gospel is really Peter's Gospel because how would have John Mark known Jesus' story without a source. He was too young to follow Jesus around, so the logical explanation was his source was Peter!

John, whose surname was Mark, was led to a saving knowledge of Jesus Christ by probably his uncle? Because of what is written above, even if not related, the famous Apostle Peter was connected to his spiritual life. Then this conversion took place we are not told by the Bible writers, but I am persuaded that it was similar to Timothy's conversion: "And that from a child thou hast known the holy scriptures, which are able to make thee wise unto salvation through faith which is in Christ Jesus." (II Timothy 3:15) If what we have already gleaned from the Biblical account is accurate then Jesus probably was a frequent visitor to Mark's home and if like we believe his parents were followers of Jesus then Mark was exposed not only to Jesus' friends but heard all about Jesus from a very young age! So it is not a stretch to understand in Peter's first epistle he would call Mark 'son'! And as we have noted in other chapters, when God uses a man or a woman to lead somebody to Himself, it is a very fitting title or term to be use!

With Uncle Barnabas, Marcus joined the first missionary team ever recorded as being sent out by a local church (Acts 13:1-4): the Antioch Church: "And when they were at Salamis, they preached the word of God in the synagogues of the Jews: **and they had also John to their minister.**" (Acts 13:5) How hard it must have been for Mark's parents to let him go? I remember when I allowed my 16-years old daughter to return with a missionary couple to Nigeria in 1996 for a three month short term mission's trip. It is not easy, but like Marnie I believe Marcus had a passion to reach the unreached with the Gospel and so when he was asked he went, yet there is not guarantee that even with the right mentors that you are spiritually or emotionally ready for such a venture! Is that what happened as we read: "Now when Paul and his company loosed from Paphos, they came to Perga in Pamphylia: and **John departing from them returned to Jerusalem.**" (Acts 13:13) No reason is given in the Acts of why Mark left the team: homesick, sacred, problems with Paul. I think most of you know that later on we read: "And some days after Paul said unto Barnabas, Let us go again and visit our brethren in every city where we have preached the word of the Lord, *and see* how they do. **And Barnabas determined to take with them John**, whose surname was Mark. But Paul thought not good to take him with them, who departed from them from Pamphylia, and went not with them to the work. And the contention was so sharp between them, that they departed asunder one from the other: and *so Barnabas took Mark*, and sailed unto Cyprus." (Acts 15:36–39)

Paul considered John Mark a spiritual dropout. Are you? How often I have known those who start a spiritual project, but never finish it! Take a Sunday School class but never finish the year. Start attending a Bible class, but never finish the course. Attend church services for a few months then drop out. Some like Jonah never get started before they drop out. I am not putting my daughter Marnie or I on a pedestal, for we both know how difficult it is to leave home and homeland young (I did it at twenty), but neither of us became a dropout, so it can be done. The good news is that this action by Mark was not the end; it was not a permanent setback to his service to the King of kings, amen!

One of the great truths about God that the Devil and many other would like for you to ignore or never know and that is the truth that we serve the God of **'the second chance'** (Jonah 3:1). And even if the Apostle Paul didn't believe it at the time Uncle Barnabas did and was willing to give Mark that chance even if Paul wouldn't. Barnabas was so convinced that Mark would make a good missionary that he was willing to break with Paul and venture out on his own with John Mark as his partner. Aren't you glad for those that have given you a second chance? Our failures in Christian service don't need to condemn us to a wasted life. I have always considered my first major ministry (a church plant in New Hampshire) a failure. I am not saying there were not some fruit, but after five years the church folded and I wondered if I would ever get a second chance. I did and in six weeks I begin my 50th year as a pastor. God not only gave me a second chance, but so did a group of believers in Aroostook County! We are never to believe Satan's lie that God has forgotten about us because we dropped out once or maybe a few times. Even at the end of John Mark's New Testament story the Apostle Paul thought differently about Marcus: "*...Take Mark, and bring him with thee: for he is profitable to me for the ministry.*" (II Timothy 4:11) All passed failures are wiped clean by forgiveness and faithfulness in the now; not only with God but with others Christians as well.

The psalmist wrote: "The steps of a *good* man are ordered by the Lord: and he delighteth in his way. Though he fall, he shall not be utterly cast down: for the Lord upholdeth *him with* his hand." (Psalm 37:23–24) Like Marcus all we have to do is confess our faults and seek a second chance like he did with Barnabas and then make good on it!

# 14

## WON: SARAH THE SEMITES
## BY: Hebrews 11:11

Through faith also Sara herself received strength to conceive seed, and was delivered of a child when she was past age, because she judged him faithful who had promised.

## ONE: ABRAM

FOR ME, WHAT IS SO amazing about Paul's statement printed above is this isn't the way it had been in Sarah's life, or at least how the Genesis account records Sarah's trust in God! The Book of Genesis records Sarah's faults, but the Book of Hebrews records her faith. As with Sarah so with us, for faults are always present before faith (Romans 3:23)!

I like what Edith Deen writes about Sarah in her book "All the Women of the Bible": "The first woman distinctly portrayed in the dramatic history of man's spiritual development is Sarah, beloved wife of Abraham, founder of the House of Israel (and prototype of the person of faith). The story of the beautiful and distinguished Sarah and her husband, 'Father of Faithful', covers more space in the Genesis account than does that of the entire human race from Creation down to their time. Sarah's life was one continuous trial of faith in God's promise that she was to be the mother of nations. Through this trial she emerged as a woman of power, one who was a dutiful and a beloved wife and who finally became a favored and venerated mother. In Sarah's period, which was probably sometime in the nineteenth or twentieth century B.C., woman assumed little importance until she had given her husband a son, for it was through his son that a man lived on. The tragedy of Sarah's early life was that she was barren, but the miracle of her life was that she gave birth to Isaac." A mighty act of God amazing grace!

As most of us know, Sarah started her Biblical experience as 'Sarai' (Genesis 11:29), Jehovah is Prince, the barren (Genesis 11:30) half-sister (Genesis 20:2) of a man named Abram from Ur. Though not mentioned must in the early story, she nevertheless followed Abram on his epic journey from Ur to Haran to Canaan to Egypt and beyond. Eventually, like her husband, God changed Sarah's name, meaning 'princess! (Genesis 17:15) We are not told in the story when Sarah put her faith in Jehovah as was with her husband (Genesis 15:6), but we get clues in the New Testament with verses like this one from the pen of Peter: "Even as Sara obeyed Abraham, calling him lord: whose daughters ye are, as long as ye do well, and are not afraid with any amazement." (I Peter 3:6) For me, this links Abram and Sarah in what we are trying to share in this book on "Won by One". What is Peter writing about when he uses Sarah as his illustration? "Likewise, ye wives, *be* in subjection to your own husbands; that, if any obey not the word, they also may without the word be won by the conversation of the wives." (I Peter 3:1) Granted, Peter was using this precept in connection of the wife leading the husband to the Lord, but we can just as well reverse the idea and speak of a husband's faith leading his wife to the Lord. I am convinced that Peter was revealing to us that it was through the defining event in Sarah's life, and that being the miraculous birth of her son in old age that also brought her to the Faith. I feel Paul writes of the same deduction with these words found in his Letter to the Romans: "And being not weak in faith, he considered not his own body now dead, when he was about an hundred years old, neither yet the deadness of Sara's womb: he staggered not at the promise of God through unbelief; but was strong in faith, giving glory to God; and being fully persuaded that, what he had promised, he was able also to perform. And therefore it was imputed to him for righteousness." (Romans 4:19–22) What Paul is doing for us is explaining the classic verse on Abram's faith: "And he believed in the LORD; and he counted it to him for righteousness." (Genesis 15:6) And I have come to believe what was written of Abram was also the process by which Sarah came to the faith, or the explanation of our key verse printed above!

The Biblical picture of Sarah begins with Sarah involved with her husband in a lie as they journey down into Egypt (Genesis 12:11). Then when the promised child doesn't show up when Abram and Sarah think he should Sarah suggests to Abram the use of her handmaid (Hagar-which she probably picked up in Egypt-one son usually results in another sin) to bear her children. (Genesis 16:1-2-a custom in those days, but we should never go to the world for the answers to our problems-they will only get us into more trouble.) Then in a jealous and merciless rage Sarah drives Hagar away after she learned she was with child (Genesis 16:6). Sarah's faults are exposed to all as her jealousy and impatience turns into lying (Genesis 18:15). Not only does she lie to God's messengers (three angels, but I believe one of them was the pre-incarnate Christ), she laughs as God's message! (Genesis 18:12) But despite her faults and failures, faith triumphed in the end as it did with me and all who eventually believe. What we always must remember is not because of HER, but because of HIM. I believe the Apostle Paul explains this concept best with these words to Timothy: "If we believe not, *yet* he abideth faithful: he cannot deny himself." (II Timothy 2:13) It might have taken 90 years, but in the end Sarah came to the Faith because of the testimony of Abram and the wondrous grace of God.

Before we leave this example of won by one, I would like for you to notice something else in the Hebrew 11 account that is unique with Sarah. Have you noticed in your reading that Paul use "By Faith" (verses 4, 5, 7, 8, 9, 17, 20, 21, 22, 23, 24, 27, 29, 30, and 31) more often, but he also uses "Through Faith" (verses 3, 11, 28, and 29). I have come to believe that 'by faith' means that through the means of faith these individuals did what they did or believed what they believed about God. However, 'through faith' means by someone else's faith they did what they did or believed what they believed in God. There is a collective faith (28, 29), but what I am referring to is the faith Sarah had didn't come from her husband, but from God Himself. Is this not what Paul is talking about in Ephesians 2:8-10: "For by grace are ye saved through faith; and that not of yourselves: *it is* the gift of God: not of works, lest any man should boast. For we are his workmanship, created in Christ Jesus unto good works, which God hath before ordained that we should walk in them." Sarah was God's 'workmanship' in that God used this doubting lady to fulfill a promise He made that through Sarah the son of promise would be given (Genesis 17:19). That is why God protected Sarah from Pharaoh (Genesis 12) and Abimelech (Genesis 20), for God had a purpose and a plan and Sarah and only Sarah was how that plan and purpose would be fulfilled! So it was God that supplied the faith and it was through faith Sarah gave birth to the Son of Promise. Again I think Peter does the best on this when he wrote: "For after this manner in **the old time the holy women also, who trusted in God**, adorned themselves, being in subjection unto their own husbands: even as Sara. . ." (I Peter 3:5–6) In the end it is all of God, so from this we must realize that even in ourselves we would be nothing and could believe nothing and accomplish nothing unless God works in us. Oh, He might use another, like Abram, to set an example before us, but that is all the 'one' can do, for in the end it is God that does the winning!

# 15

## WON: RUTH THE MOABITESS
## BY: Ruth 1:16

And Ruth said, Intreat me not to leave thee, *or* to return from following after thee: for whither thou goest, I will go; and where thou lodgest, I will lodge: thy people *shall be* my people, and thy God my God.

## ONE: NAOMI

FOR ME, WHAT MAKES the Ruth story so amazing and another marvelous example of God's mercy and grace is this commandment from Moses' law: "An Ammonite or **Moabite** shall not enter into the congregation of the LORD; even to their tenth generation shall they not enter into the congregation of the LORD for ever." (Deuteronomy 23:3) Ponder this rule for a moment before you think about Ruth the Moabitess. This puts to rest the misconception and myth that grace is only a New Testament concept, for if this were the only Old Testament story on grace it would still be enough to debunk the myth and counteract the misconception. It also verifies again the precept we have been highlighting and underling in this book "Won by One" and that being: "Then Peter opened *his* mouth, and said, Of a truth I perceive that God is no respecter of persons: but ***in every nation*** he that feareth him, and worketh righteousness, is accepted with him." (Acts 10:34-35) And finally, we see again the Almighty using a human being in his marvellous plan of salvation, and this time it is the widow Naomi!

The story of Ruth begins in the happy days of marriage, yet even in this we observe another clearly defined commanded in the Mosaic Law:

"Neither shalt thou make marriages with them; thy daughter thou shalt not give unto his son, nor his daughter shalt thou take unto thy son." (Deuteronomy 7:3) It was one thing to leave the Promised Land in a time of famine (Ruth 1:1), but to marry their (Elimelech and Naomi) sons to Moabite girls (Ruth 1:4) was condemned. All seemed to be well for ten years then the Hand of God began to work His ultimate purpose. In time 3 funerals happened in Moab leaving three widows destitute and alone (Ruth 1:30). It was then that Naomi decided that it was best to return to Israel where she had relatives, but what to do with her two daughters-in-laws? She knew the Law and that the prospect of remarriage to another Jewish man in Israel wouldn't happen, so she encouraged Ruth and Orpah to stay in their homeland where they might find another husband. It appears they all started for Israel (Ruth 1:8-13), but during their walk the conversation eventually persuaded Orpah to turn back, but of Ruth it says: "And they lifted up their voice, and wept again: and Orpah kissed her mother in law; **but Ruth clave unto her.**" (Ruth 1:14) What is revealing to me is the argument of Naomi to Ruth: "And she said, Behold, thy sister in law is gone back unto her people, **and unto her gods**: return thou after thy sister in law." (Ruth 1:15) I feel this is the moment for Ruth's great decision, for no matter Naomi's arguments Ruth insisted in accompanying Naomi back to Bethlehem and in so doing placed herself on a course to become one of the noblest women of the Bible, Jewish history, and 'won by one'!

Despite Ruth's background: from a cursed race, a young widow, and desperately poor, she shines as a ruby without price: "Who can find a virtuous woman? for her price *is* far above rubies." (Proverbs 31:10) Ruth typifies the qualities God is always looking for in a woman: "Whose adorning let it not be that outward *adorning* of plaiting the hair, and of wearing of gold, or of putting on of apparel; but *let it be* the hidden man of the heart, in that which is not corruptible, *even the ornament* of a meek and quiet spirit, which is in the sight of God of great price." (I Peter 3:3-4) So what are these characteristics that we can see in Ruth that I feel she first saw in Naomi, the 'one' of our story of 'won':

1. ***First Ruth's Charity.*** (Ruth 1:16) Not only was Ruth willing to give up her heritage, but her religion as well. Through Naomi not only had Ruth learned to love another family, but also another faith. I feel in the end she was not cleaving to Naomi, but Naomi's God, Jehovah. Edith Deen writes in her book "All the Women of the Bible": "Like

so many young widows, she might have said, 'somebody else must take care of this forlorn woman. I'm still young I want to marry again. The mother of my first husband is in my way!' But Ruth made another choice, and she made it gracefully." I believe like Deen that Ruth had fallen in love with Naomi, a loveless mother maybe, but the great love of God is seen when we show love to others, even a mother-in-law! Read I John 4:17–21.

2. *Second Ruth's Constancy.* (Ruth 1:18) Orpah started for Bethlehem but turned back, Ruth continued. When things got rough in Bethlehem; not once did Ruth consider going back to Moab. Ruth had set her course and as Jesus would teach years later: "And Jesus said unto him, No man, having put his hand to the plough, and looking back, is fit for the kingdom of God." (Luke 9:62) A quality rare today in women; Deen continues: "She never altered from her unselfish purpose during the many trials that followed. Nor did she ever complain because she had given up everything, her country, and her relationships with young friends, or her chance to marry a man in her own country. She had given them all up with the resolution fierce in its quietness!" Read the Book of Ruth and see this to be true.

3. *Third Ruth's Piety.* (Ruth 1:17) I believe this follow-up verse from our key verse teaches us that Ruth was resting her future in the Will of God. Naomi hadn't given her a false-hope in a future marriage (Ruth 1:11–13), and I believe Ruth was still very young. There might have been hope in Moab, but Bethlehem? I believe this piety of faith was first in Naomi, despite Naomi's periods of depression (Ruth 1:19–22), and whether or not Naomi knew it her testimony had won in the end!

4. *Forth Ruth's Industry.* (Ruth 2:6, 7, and 23) A willing worker in a woman is to be honored and admired. Again read Proverbs 31 on the qualities of the virtuous woman and you will see that 'industry' is underlined time and time again. I believe this was the first quality that Boaz saw in Ruth, love would come later! Ruth was not lazy. Ruth was not found sulking over her poor estate or prospects. Ruth was not self-centered and proud that she wouldn't get her hands dirty. Ruth took responsibility for her and her mother-in-law's need. That is why in the end they said to Naomi: "And he shall be unto thee a restorer of *thy* life, and a nourisher of thine old age: for

thy daughter in law, which loveth thee, which is better to thee than seven sons, hath born him." (Ruth 4:15) Amen and Amen!

5. **Fifth Ruth's Conformability.** (Ruth 3:5) Ruth adapted. Ruth was changeable. Ruth was not so set in her ways that she couldn't conform to what God was doing in her life. The result was this testimonial of Ruth by her future husband: "And now, my daughter, fear not; I will do to thee all that thou requirest: for all the city of my people doth know that thou *art* a virtuous woman." (Ruth 3:11) This is why in the end, Ruth would become the wife of Boaz (Ruth4:13), the grandmother of David (Ruth 4:22), and a part of the Messianic story (Matthew 1:5) of the Christ!

# 16

## WON: THE CALVARY THIEF
## BY: Luke 23:42

And he said unto Jesus, Lord, remember me
when thou comest into thy kingdom.

## ONE: JESUS

To my knowledge the Bible only records one 'death-bed' conversion story: the thief on the cross. Some would consider the Philippian jailer (see chapter 12) in the same position seeing he was only moments from taking his own life when he cried" "Sirs, what must I do to be saved?" (Acts 16:31) The jailer survived his near-death experience because of the truth of Paul and Silas' answer to his question: "And they said, Believe on the Lord Jesus Christ, and thou shalt be saved, and thy house." (Acts 16:31) On the other hand, the thief died within hours of his conversion, but everlasting life was his through Christ's redemption. For those of us who have spent their lives ministering to people in 'the last mile of the way', it is a great comfort to us that God's mercy and grace extends to those final hours, minutes, or seconds I believe. Those of us who stand near the doors of hell are comforted that at the last moment people still can get converted and escape an eternity from the presence of God. The story of the thief on the cross is an acknowledgment that despite wasting a lifetime in sin, God's grace does reach to the last second, and when the opportunity is give a person has a choice. I find the two thieves an excellent illustration of the two choices everybody has to the last day, the last mile, and the last moment. For we know that salvation happens in a moment, just like the malefactor's miracle when he was 'won by one' and that One was the Lord Himself!

His name and the details of his crime are absent from the account in the Gospel according to Luke, for I believe neither are necessary for the truth of the story. I have come to believe one of the reasons that many names are missing from Holy Writ, and sin details are also missing is to give to us an example that can fit anyone of us. The great word on this is 'whosoever' (Romans 10:13) and 'all' (Romans 3:23). That covers everyone and everything in connection to sin and sinners! The key however to both is this from the thief's own lips: "And we indeed justly; for we receive the due reward of our deeds: but this man hath done nothing amiss." (Luke 23:41) What a contrast from the lips of the other thief, on Jesus' other side: "And one of the malefactors which were hanged railed on him, saying, If thou be Christ, save thyself and us." (Luke 23:39) Even the converted thief recognized the difference: "But the other answering rebuked him, saying, Dost not thou fear God, seeing thou art in the same condemnation?" (Luke 23:40) Years ago I saw that in these three crucified ones we have the full picture of what is the greatest decision of our lives. In the arrogant thief we have an example of *'the man dying in his sins'*! In the converted thief we have the example of *'the man who died to his sins'*! And the man on the middle cross is *'the man who died for all sin'*! And why do I believe that the thief of Calvary got saved that moment through the example of Jesus Christ and because of Jesus Christ? It all has to do with what Jesus said to him after his confession and request: "And Jesus said unto him, Verily I say unto thee, To day shalt thou be with me in paradise." (Luke 23:43) This is the promise of everlasting life (Romans 6:23)!

All the key ingredients are in this conversion story to prove to me that the thief was saved at the last moment. Remember Jesus' precept of Matthew 7:20: "Wherefore by their fruits ye shall know them." Granted, Jesus was talking about the fruits of the false teachers, but there are also fruits of salvation that need to be seen in each convert. I like to call them the ABC's of Salvation. First, the thief **acknowledged** that he was a sinner (Luke 23:41). "For all have sinned, and come short of the glory of God." (Romans 3:23) Second, the thief **believed** that Jesus could save him. (Luke 23:42) "But as many as received him, to them gave he power to become the sons of God, *even* to them that believe on his name." (John 1:12) And Third, the thief **confessed** Christ privately to God and publicly to man. (Luke 23:42) "Whosoever therefore shall confess me before men, him will I confess also before my Father which is in heaven." (Matthew

10:32) For me, Romans 10:9-10 summarizes these three precepts; check them out!

I believe moments away from hell's fire, the thief's soul was plucked from the flames and sent to Paradise; to Abraham's bosom instead of Apollyon's bowels, to Paradise not Purgatory. While the crowed was shouting "Save Thyself!" (Luke 23:35), the thief was saying save me. While the other thief was shouting "Save Thyself and Us!" (Luke 23:39) the thief was shouting save me. The Philippian jail asked what must *"I"*; personal. Until salvation becomes personal there will be no salvation. This thief took his final chance and laid claim to Paradise through a dying man on a cross! As I have already said; it is my interpretation that the thief died within hours. I know Jesus died first, but remember in order to quicken their deaths Pilate gave permission for their legs to be broken. They didn't break Jesus' legs because he was already died, but what of the thieves? (John 19:31-37) I also believe that the moment the thief did expire he was immediately transported to Paradise where Jesus was already there waiting for him. Similar to how Paul described it for the believer after Jesus' resurrection: "We are confident, *I say*, and willing rather to be absent from the body, and to be present with the Lord." (II Corinthians 5:8) Paul would also write: "For to me to live *is* Christ, and to die *is* gain." (Philippians 1:21) I expect that the thief though the same thing when he opened his eyes in Paradise and in the presence of Jesus; while the other thief like the rich man lifted up his eyes in hell and saw afar off, like Lazarus, his partner in crime talking to Jesus. Read carefully Luke 16:19-26 for a better description of what I feel happened. The decision to believe in Jesus from a cross changed the eternal destiny and destination of this thief!

What a miracle from the brow of Calvary's hill. I believe the song writer John W. Peterson said it best in these lines: "It took a miracle to put the stars in place. It took a miracle to hang the world in space. But when He saved my soul, cleansed and made me whole; it took a miracle of love and grace!" Today, everybody will have to make a decision about the Christ sooner or later. Granted, you might like the thieves wait to the last moment to be confronted with what Jesus did for you on Calvary, but a choice you will make, and when you make no choice you have made a choice. In the end it will come down to what you decided about what Jesus did! Won't you cry 'save me' before it is too late. Remember the rich man couldn't change his earthly choice even when from hell he recognized Lazarus and Abraham. I believe the thief that rejected Jesus on earth recognized Him from hell. That is why we must take this admonition from the pen of Paul: "(For he saith, I have heard thee in a time accepted, and in the day of salvation have I succoured thee: behold, now *is* the accepted time; behold, now *is* the day of salvation.)" (II Corinthians 6:2) Whoever you are, whatever kind of person you are, the invitation that was given to the thief is still open to you. Remember, you don't need another human being because all you need is the best 'won by one' individual in the business: Jesus!

# 17

## WON: PETER THE GALILAEAN
## BY: John 1:41

He first findeth his own brother Simon, and saith unto him, We have found the Messias, which is, being interpreted, the Christ.

## ONE: ANDREW

WE HAVE BEFORE US in this chapter a classic example of our "won by one" precept. We also have before us one of the most significant soul winning efforts in history, for without this conversion the Church of the Living God would have turned out quite differently. Andrew doesn't get as much press or is not mentioned in a sermon as much as Peter, but without 'the little fisherman' there never would have been 'the Big Fisherman'!

When I think of Andrew I think of all the unsung heroes and heroines of Church history that lived in the shadow of the people that brought them to Christ in the first place. Who lead Dwight Lyman Moody, better known at D.L. Moody to the Lord? Moody would become one of the greatest soul winners in Church history, but who led him to Christ. On April 21, 1855, Moody was brought to a saving knowledge of Christ by Edward Kimball. Most would say who is Edward Kimball? Kimball was a Sunday school teacher who believed in sharing his faith both in the class room and in any other room he found himself in. On that day Kimball was in a shoe store in Boston where Moody was clerking. Few know the Kimball story, or even know his name, but what a catch for Christ Kimball had that day. Which of us knows whether or not the next person we share our faith with might just be the one the Good Lord is going to change the world with, or in the case of Peter: 'turn the world upside down' with! (Acts 17:6) Little did Kimball or Andrew know on that meaningful day the effect their witness would have on history!

Andrew also reminds me of the importance of seeking our own. Remember what Jesus said to the man he had cast out 'a legion of demon' (Mark 5:18). After his conversion this unnamed man wanted to travel with Jesus and tell his amazing story of conversion, but Jesus had a different purpose for him: "Howbeit Jesus suffered him not, but saith unto him, Go home to thy friends, and tell them how great things the Lord hath done for thee, and hath had compassion on thee." (Mark 5:19) So when Andrew had meet Jesus his first concern was for the lost estate of his brother Simon! Like Andrew I believe our first missionfield is home; this is our "Jerusalem" in the great commission (Acts 1:8). I have come to believe they might be the hardest to reach, for I have found I have had far more success in sharing the Gospel to strangers verses friends! But like Andrew we must 'first find'. And when we find that someone the Lord has lain on your heart; you are to do like Andrew and simply tell them your story, a testimonial to how you meet Jesus, and then we simply let the Holy Spirit do the rest. There is no doubt from the context that Simon was moved because he also wanted to see Jesus: "And he brought him to Jesus. And when Jesus beheld him, he said, Thou art Simon the son of Jona: thou shalt be called Cephas, which is by interpretation, A stone." (John 1:42) It is not in John's Gospel, but in Matthew's Gospel we get the clearest declaration of faith by Peter: "And Simon Peter answered and said, Thou art the Christ, the Son of the living God." (Matthew 16:16) But who was it that introduced Simon to the Saviour; his brother Andrew. I would challenge you to trace the life of Andrew and discover as I have that every time Andrew is mentioned as a key character in a story he is always being someone to the Christ!

Simon Peter is a wonderful example of what Christ can do with a life that is turned over to him. I believe that when Peter first met Jesus that he was a foolish man building his life on sand, but after Jesus got through molding him he was the wise man who built his life on a rock (Matthew 7:24–27), and that Rock was Jesus (I Corinthians 10:4). As I concluded however, it was a constant struggle of Simonizing verses Peterizing. A simple study of Peter's biography in Scripture sees the shifting sand character that characterized Simon's early years with Christ. Remember Peter vowed he would never deny Jesus; that Jesus would never wash his feet; that Jesus would not die; that he could walk on water, yet within moments of those boasts he did just the opposite. I have come to believe that Simon was the man James talked about: "A double minded man *is* unstable in all his ways." (James 1:8) Simon's sleepiness in the Garden is another example of the fact that Peter was still being worked on, and for those who thank that Pentecost changed everything the tendency for Peter being Simonized; Peter always had trouble with Simon: "But when Peter was come to Antioch, I withstood him to the face, because he was to be blamed. For before that certain came from James, he did eat with the Gentiles: but when they were come, he withdrew and separated himself, fearing them which were of the circumcision." (Galatians 2:11–12) Here Peter feared the rebuke of the Jews in his association with the Gentiles, and so will we fight the old nature all our lives.

Despite Peter's unstable character, his speaking often before he thought and his shifting sand character, the Lord saw a tremendous potential in Simon from the beginning. When Jesus gave Simon his new name it wasn't a declaration of what Simon was, but what Simon would become. I think that was the same with Gideon when the angel upon his first visit said: "...thou mighty man of valour..." (Judges 6:12) If you know the story Gideon wasn't acting like a mighty man of valour at the time, but in time he would be (Judges 7–8). So instead of a Simon Jesus was going to make a Peter out of him. Instead of sand, a stone. I believe that is possible for each of us because of Ephesians 2:10: "For we are his workmanship, created in Christ Jesus unto good works, which God hath before ordained that we should walk in them." Christ's goal with Simon was to Peterize Simon. One warning before we go on and that is something Jesus said to Simon before Gethsemane: "And the Lord said, Simon, Simon, behold, Satan hath desired *to have* you, that he may sift *you* as wheat." (Luke 22:31) So will Jesus was Peterizing Simon, Satan was trying to Simonize Peter; and he will with us as well!

Have you been changed after your conversion? Remember this from the pen of Paul: "Therefore if any man *be* in Christ, *he is* a new creature: old things are passed away; behold, all things are become new." (II Corinthians 5:17) Since childhood I have known the chorus: "He's still working on me to make me what I ought to be!" Peter the Galilaean (Luke 22:59) is the classic example for so many of the common precepts we have been trying to highlight and underline in this book. Surely we see that he was won to Christ through the intervention of his brother Andrew, but he is also the example of the man who came as he was and then he allowed the Christ to change him, reshape him into Christ's own image (Romans

8:29). Peter is a wonderful example of the potter and the clay principle of Jeremiah 18:6: "O house of Israel, cannot I do with you as this potter? saith the LORD. Behold, as the clay *is* in the potter's hand, so *are* ye in mine hand, O house of Israel." When will we be able to convince people that they are exactly what God is looking for (I Corinthians 1:26–29). Our job is to tell them, 'the great changer' can remold anyone into what He wants them to be, but like with Andrew we must find them!

# 18

## WON: CORNELIUS THE ITALIAN
## BY: Acts 10:1-2

There was a certain man in Caesarea called Cornelius, a centurion of the band called the Italian *band*, a devout *man*, and one that feared God with all his house, which gave much alms to the people, and prayed to God always.

## ONE: PETER

MOST MIGHT BE SURPRISED to learn that Cornelius, though famous and recognized by most who know their Bible is actually only mentioned once in the Scriptures! Despite his fame as being known as the first Gentile (first named Gentile convert to Christianity, for there is ample proof that he wasn't the first Gentile to believe in Jesus-consider John 12:20-22 and Acts 2:10) convert recorded as having accepted the truth concerning the Christ, yet his name only appears in the text of his conversion (Acts 10). For me, Cornelius is another great example for the premise of this book: "Won by One".

The ingredients for a first chance conversion must begin with seeking God first. Remember how Cornelius testimony began. (see above) I have preached for years that a seeking Saviour (Luke 19:10) will always find a seeking sinner. Certainly Cornelius wasn't saved simple because he was a 'devout man', a 'God fearing man', a 'giving man', or a 'praying man'! Remember what Isaiah wrote: "But we are all as an unclean *thing*, and all our righteousnesses *are* as filthy rags; and we all do fade as a leaf; and our iniquities, like the wind, have taken us away." (Isaiah 64:6) This was just a preparation for his conversion, but I have found that men God has found are often alone just like Cornelius was alone seeking God. Remember Moses (Exodus 3:1–5), Gideon (Judges 6:11), Jephthah (Judges 11:29), Joshua (Joshua 5:13), and Jacob (Genesis 32:24) were all alone when they really meet God for the first time. You must be able to say with Matthew's description of the final moments of the transfiguration of Jesus: "And when they had lifted up their eyes, they saw no man, save Jesus only." (Matthew 17:8) I have often wondered if my aloneness as a child was the reason that I too was converted so young (7 years of age) and quickly (a Sunday morning at a children's church service).

After alone to hear God, the next step is attentiveness to God: "He saw in a vision evidently about the ninth hour of the day an angel of God coming in to him, and saying unto him, Cornelius." (Acts 10:3) God will call, but will you listen, or are you listening? Remember the story of Samuel (I Samuel 3:1–10). Eli had to teach Samuel to listen to God, and sometimes we must be taught, but we know from the rest of the story of Cornelius, he was listening, because God loves the single, lost sheep (Matthew 18:11–14). The reason that Cornelius was soon found is the precept I have already shared above, but worth repeating again: a soul-seeking Lord and a shepherd seeking a sheep will always find a calling sheep! I have discovered in nearly fifty years as a shepherd (pastor) that most people miss the Lord's calling, not because the Lord is not calling, but because the person is not listening. I have witness the truth that there is no force in heaven or in earth that can keep a seeking sinner from a seeking Saviour. God was seeking Cornelius' soul, and Cornelius was searching to understand God better. I believe that Cornelius had already converted to Judaism: he was a proselyte. What I find interesting is that they found each other in the presents of seven skeptical saints: "And the Spirit bade me go with them, nothing doubting. Moreover these six brethren accompanied me, and we entered into the man's house." (Acts 11:12) (In Peter testimony to the Church of what happened at Cornelius' house.) Read how surprised they actually were in Acts 10:45!

I believe in the precept of 'ready to receive'. To close one's mind and heart to the moving of the Holy Spirit (John 16:8) will have eternal consequences, but to open up one's heart and mind to the moving of the Holy Spirit results in a first chance conversion. At Berea, Paul and Silas found a people according to Moffatt's Translation of the New Testament that ". . .were perfectly ready to receive the Word. . ." (Acts 17:11) I say this too the honor and glory of the eternal God that I feel I responded and got gloriously saved on my first chance at salvation. I am not saying that from an early age I didn't hear the Good News for I was raised in a family of believers that shared the truth about Jesus and I went early to a church that taught the same thing, but when I felt the moving of the Holy Spirit for the first time I accepted the fact that I was a sinner and that Jesus died for my sins on Calvary's tree and by believing in Him I got saved. I turned 71 a few months ago and since that first day to this day I have known the Lord.

The final ingredient to a first chance conversion is the fear of the Lord: "And when he looked on him, he was afraid, and said, what is it, Lord? And he said unto him, Thy prayers and thine alms are come up for a memorial before God." (Acts 10:4) We have stopped teaching this precept because we think it is only an Old Testament concept: "The fear of the Lord *is* the beginning of wisdom: and the knowledge of the holy *is* understanding." (Proverbs 9:10) Is there a greater wisdom than the truth of salvation and is there a greater understanding than knowing how to get salvation? The modern Church has stopped preaching on hell, damnation, and the Lake of Fire. We have decided that to scare or bring fear in the heart of people is wrong and yet Jesus preached more about hell than he did about heaven. Our theology about God has changed, and with it a respect and reverence and the fear of the Lord has been changed to God being someone you pat on the back, you shake His hand, and say how it is going God! Not so in the days of Cornelius, and even John who had been a disciple and friend of Jesus years before is recorded of having done this when Jesus meet him again on the Island of Patmos: "And when I saw him, I fell at his feet as dead. And he laid his right hand upon me, saying unto me, Fear not; I am the first and the last." (Revelation 1:17) Note the respect and reverence; granted Jesus said not to fear, but He wasn't taking about a Proverbs 1:7 kind of fear. I believe Cornelius got saved because he had a healthy respect for God, and Cornelius got saved at a moment's notice after Peter had shared with him the Good News about Jesus Christ (Acts 10:34–43). Though Jonathan Edwards would preach his famous sermon, "Sinner in the Hands of an Angry God", 1700 years after Peter's message to Cornelius and family, the tone was the same. I was raised to respect and reverence the Almighty and I believe it was a factor in my early conversion.

Has your first chance passed? Actually few people get converted on their first conviction, but I have some more good news for you. The God of our salvation is also the God of the second chance (Jonah 3:1), and for some many, many more chances. But just maybe the reading of this chapter has stirred in you to remembrance a time you said "no" to God, but that He is still tugging at your hearts strings. He is still standing at the door of your heart and knocking. Are you alone today, are you attentive today, and are you afraid that your time is running out? If you are alive you still have time, and whether alone or you need a Peter to share with you; Cornelius is still a great example of 'won by one'!

# 19

## WON: ZACCHAEUS THE JERICHOITE
## BY: Luke 19:9

And Jesus said unto him, this day is salvation come to this house, forsomuch as he also is a son of Abraham.

## ONE: JESUS

ONE OF THE MORE interesting things to me in the ministry of Jesus Christ where the different places people got saved; but we would all agree that there is only one way to get saved: ". . .Believe on the Lord Jesus Christ and thou shalt be saved. . ." (Acts 16:31) Would we agree that there is only one name whereby we are saved? "Neither is there salvation in any other, for there is none other name under heaven given among men whereby we must be saved." (Acts 4:12) But when it comes to where we can be saved the places are as varied as the people who do get saved; even though there are those that believe a sacred place is needed, or a holy river! The Bible tells us that a Samaritan woman got saved by a well drawing water (John 4:7). The Bible also tells us that an Ethiopian eunuch got saved in a chariot in a desert place. (Acts 8:27) Nicodemus got saved at night (John 3:1) and Paul got saved at high noon on a road (Acts 9:3). You name a place or a circumstance and probably somebody got saved then and there. I will never forget the story told by Maine evangelist Wendell Calder about the boy who got saved in a manure pile. Convicted by a sermon he had heard the night before, he literally fell on his knees while removing dung from a cow barn to a manure pile. He returned to the special meeting being held in his father's church that evening and told Wendell all about it. It is not where you get saved that counts, but how you get saved that is the important thing. We are told that Jesus left the Spirit to '. . .reprove the world of sin. . .' (John 16:8) and he can do that in a person's heart at any moment and anywhere! The only question is will the person respond to the conviction because people say "no" like Felix: "And as he reasoned of righteousness, temperance, and judgment to come, Felix trembled, and answered, go thy way for this time; when I have a convenient season, I will call for thee." (Acts 24:25) Putting it off is a "no" because often there is no other 'convenient season'. What about King Herod Agrippa? "Then Agrippa said unto Paul, Almost thou persuadest me to be a Christian." (Acts 26:28) This is also a rejection because 'almost' only counts in horseshoes. Convictions shouldn't be squandered because according to Isaiah 55:6 there might not be another time: "Seek ye the LORD while he may be found, call ye upon him while he is near." Our 'won by one' hero in this chapter took advantage of the Spirit's conviction and got saved in another strange place: in a tree!

I am not fully convinced that when Zacchaeus woke that morning in Jericho that he was thinking about salvation, or this would be the day his world would be turned upside down? I am convinced that Zacchaeus woke that morning the richest man in town, but before the day was finished he would be one of the poorest. I am fully persuaded that Zacchaeus woke that morning with the reputation that he was the greediest man in town, and yet before the day was through he would be known as the most generous man in town. I am also convinced that Zacchaeus was one of the shortest men in Jericho, but before Jesus got through with him he would be one of the tallest. Yes, Zacchaeus began his day thinking of how much tax money he could take from his fellow Jerichoites and how he could steal and cheat the Romans out of their share of the tax profits generated in this important commercial town. But somewhere between his fancy house on the city of palms and his fabulous office downtown something eternal happened to our rich man, and it all took place because 'the seeker of souls' (John 19:10) was passing through!

The story begins with these very important words: "And *Jesus* entered and passed through Jericho." (Luke 19:1) I love John 4:4 in the Samaritan Woman story: "And he must needs go through Samaria." I think the same of Jericho. There was a lone soul there that needed salvation. These two stories teach us the wonderful truth of this statement from Jesus that publicans (Zacchaeus) and harlots (the woman) would get into the kingdom of God. It also underlines and highlights again the precept that we have shared many times in this book: "Then Peter opened *his* mouth, and said, of a truth I perceive that God is no respecter of persons: but in every nation he that feareth him, and worketh righteousness, is accepted with him." (Acts 10:34-35) Zacchaeus didn't know it when he left home, but he was on his way to an appointment that wasn't in his daily planner, and this rendezvous would change his life, his walk, his way of doing things, and his eternal destination. Zacchaeus started that morning on the road to Hell, but ended the day on the narrow road that leads to Heaven; and it all started at a sycamore tree.

Because of Zacchaeus' stature he couldn't see through the crowd that had gathered to see this man from Galilee come through their town. Jesus was famous by now and the crowds always followed, but in the typical bandwagon affect Zacchaeus got caught in the crowd on his way to work. He wanted to see what all the commotion was about, so he climbed a tree on the road Jesus was using to pass through. Salvation often begins with a curious inquisitiveness. Surely Zacchaeus had to shallow a bit of pride, but his interest got the best of him and it says: "And he ran before, and climbed up into a sycamore tree to see him: for he was to pass that *way.*" (Luke 19:4) I believe Zacchaeus was born in Jericho and he knew of the tree on the way, so he was ready to see this Jesus, but he wasn't ready for what Jesus did when He got to the tree: "And when Jesus came to the place, he looked up, and saw him, and said unto him, Zacchaeus, make haste, and come down; for to day I must abide at thy house." (Luke 19:5) When you have a seeking Saviour, He will find you wherever you are even if you're 'up a tree and out on a limb'. How do I know Jesus knew Zacchaeus? Because He called him by name, and we know that Jesus wasn't just passing through but expected to stop at Zacchaeus' house! I believe that before Zacchaeus feet hit the ground he was saved, and the proof was in what he told Jesus: "And Zacchaeus stood, and said unto the Lord; Behold, Lord, the half of my goods I give to the poor; and if I have taken any thing from any man by false accusation, I restore *him* fourfold." (Luke 19:8) Salvation brings change, and what a change took place in the heart of the publican from Jericho that day!

What will you do with Jesus' invitation? Zacchaeus could have stayed in the tree like Agrippa and Felix without any spiritual hope, but praise God he didn't. I see in this story three important things that must take place in all conversion: 1) **Zacchaeus obeyed immediately** (Luke 19:6-check John 10:4). 2) **Zacchaeus rejoiced joyfully** (Luke 19:6-check Romans 5:2). 3) **Zacchaeus changed dramatically** (Luke 19:8-check II

Corinthians 5:17) Zacchaeus' conversion is a classic illustration of our Won by One precept as Jesus shows us again the importance of meeting people where they are. Only when we allow the Holy Spirit to direct will we be at the right place at the right time to say the right thing to the right person. Also Zacchaeus teaches us: "How shall we escape, if we neglect so great salvation; which at the first began to be spoken by the Lord. . ." (Hebrews 2:3) He is after you where you are!

# 20

## WON: THE CAPERNAUM CENTURIAN
## BY: Matthew 8:10

When Jesus heard *it*, he marvelled, and said to them that followed, Verily I say unto you, I have not found so great faith, no, not in Israel.

## ONE: JESUS

"Jesus came and spake unto them, saying, All power is given unto me in heaven and in earth." (Matthew 28:18) And when Jesus said this at the end of His ministry; He had proven through His ministry that this statement was true! One of my favorite chapters in the Gospel according to Matthew illustrates and underlines just what kind of power was given to the Christ here on earth. First we see Jesus' power over the dreaded disease of leprosy (Matthew 8:1–4). Second we see Jesus' power over the distant (Jesus didn't have to be there to heal) disease of the centurion's servant (Matthew 8:5–13). Third we see Jesus' power over daily diseases like the one that afflicted Peter's mother-in-law (Matthew 8:14–15). Fourth we see Jesus' power over the diverse disease found in the crowds that flocked to Jesus (Matthew 8:16–17). Fifth we see Jesus' power the disciple's disease that kept certain would-be disciples from following after the Christ (Matthew 8:18–22). Sixth we see Jesus' power over the disease of doubt that broke out among the disciples on the Sea of Galilee when a terrible storm almost sunk their boat (Matthew 8:23–27) And seventh we see Jesus' power over the demonic disease that afflicted the man from Gergesenes (Matthew 8:28–34). But for me the greatest power that Jesus demonstrated was the power to save men's souls as He did with the centurion of Capernaum when He gave the greatest tribute He ever gave to anyone during His ministry: ". . .I have not found so great faith, no, not in Israel!" At a moment's notice this foreigner but his trust in a man he had never meet, and gave to us another example of 'won by one' and a great precept in the ongoing understanding of 'faith'!

What does it take to have 'great faith'? I believe this Roman soldier had all the ingredients to help us define 'great faith', a term that is rarely used in the Bible. I would have you first notice that it is not dependent on race or religion. This man was a Roman by race and a heathen by religion. A centurion was a Roman officer with a hundred men under him; the basic element in the well-organized Roman Army. This personal servant that he loved was probably a slave that had been raised with him from childhood as a personal servant. Our story begins with these words: "And when Jesus was entered into Capernaum, there came unto him a centurion, beseeching him, and saying, Lord, my servant lieth at home sick of the palsy, grievously tormented." (Matthew 8:5-6) I think we must note here that it takes great compassion to have great faith. One of my favorite Christians of all time was Hudson Taylor, the great Church missionary to China. If you read of his life you will conclude with me that he was a man of great faith for China because he had a great compassion for the souls of the Chinese. Taylor once wrote this to his mother: "Think of the twelve million, a number so great that it is impossible to realize it. Yes, twelve mission souls in China every year passing without God and without hope of eternity. Oh, let us look with compassion on this multitude!" Whether 12,000,000 or one it takes 'compassion' to have great faith and remember this was said of Jesus: "But when he saw the multitudes, he was moved with compassion on them, because they fainted, and were scattered abroad, as sheep having no shepherd." (Matthew 9:36)

Following the centurion's request: "And Jesus saith unto him, I will come and heal him." (Matthew 8:7) I believe after compassion one must have great trust in the promises of God to have 'great faith'. Paul put it best in II Corinthians 1:20: "For all the promises of God in him *are* yea, and in him Amen, unto the glory of God by us." Long before this centurion claimed this promise he was practicing this instruction by the pen of Peter: "Whereby are given unto us exceeding great and precious promises: that by these ye might be partakers of the divine nature. . ." (II Peter 1:4) "Great faith" is part of the divine nature and this centurion had it as did Hudson Taylor. Hudson Taylor's faith developed into great faith according to his son (Dr. Howard Taylor) in his book about his father called

"Hudson Taylor's Spiritual Secrets" because "Above all, he (Taylor) put to test the promises of God, and felt he must not lose the opportunity of further testing the promises of God." Like Hudson, the Roman centurion was quick to put Jesus' promise to the test, but in a way few try. I have come to believe that faith can only grow if it is tried and tested, so when we are confronted with a trial we need to like this centurion use it to see how far we can apply our faith; for great faith only comes when tested!

The reaction of the centurion to the Lord's willingness to come immediately and heal his servant to some seems strange, but now that we know that 'great faith' was being demonstrated it isn't as strange: "The centurion answered and said, Lord, I am not worthy that thou shouldest come under my roof: but speak the word only, and my servant shall be healed." (Matthew 8:8) So after compassion and trusting God's promises we see great humility demonstrated by this soldier. So many people came to Jesus thinking they were doing Jesus a favor, but not this centurion. He immediately recognized that Jesus was superior to him (remember the Romans were in Israel occupying the land, a superior people controlling an inferior people). Read the story of the publican and the Pharisee again (Luke 18:9–13). I loved Hudson Taylor's answer to a question to why he went to China as a missionary, and I quote: "One day the Lord came to me and said, my child I am going to evangelize inland China, and if you would like to walk with Me I will do it through you!" Now that is great humility. So many love the glory and the credit, but God is looking for people who He can get glory through (read I Corinthians 1:26–29).

So my understanding of 'great faith' is that it is breed in the heart and mind of someone with great compassion for others, great trust in God's promises, and great humility of character. This is why I believe Jesus found great faith in that centurion that day, and why he accepted the centurions reasoning: "For I am a man under authority, having soldiers under me: and I say to this *man*, Go, and he goeth; and to another, Come, and he cometh; and to my servant, Do this, and he doeth *it*." (Matthew 8:9) It has to do with our belief in the authority of God! I don't believe a man starts out with 'great faith'. Over the years I have found this pattern of faith in the Scriptures: "no faith' (Mark 4:40); "little faith" (Luke 12:28); "rich faith" (James 2:5); "precious faith" (II Peter 1:1); "great faith" (Matthew 8:10), "full faith" (Acts 6:5), and "perfect faith" (James 2:22). Paul wrote this: "Night and day praying exceedingly that we might see your face, and might perfect that which is lacking in your faith?" (I Thessalonians 3:10) And "We are bound to thank God always for you, brethren, as it is meet, because that your faith groweth exceedingly, and the charity of every one of you all toward each other aboundeth." (II Thessalonians 1:3) Are you cultivating the seed of faith in your heart and is it growing?

# 21

**WON**: ANDREW THE FISHERMAN
**BY**: John 1:40
One of the two which heard John *speak*, and followed him, was Andrew, Simon Peter's brother.

**ONE**: JOHN THE BAPTIST

Jesus was the original 'fisher-of-men', and in turn he created others that would fish for men as well. I believe it all has to do with this precept from the pen of Paul: "And the things that thou hast heard of me among many witnesses, the same commit thou to faithful men, who shall be able to teach others also." (II Timothy 2:2) Like with baptism, a practice that would become an important element even in Jesus' ministry, even though He Himself didn't baptize (John 4:1–2), but would become a sacrament in the early church (Acts 2:41), so with fishing for men both were started by John the Baptist, and one of John's first catches was Andrew the fisherman. Originally a disciple of John things would change one day with these words: "Again the next day after John stood, and two (Andrew and John) of his disciples; and looking upon Jesus as he walked, he saith, Behold the Lamb of God!" (John 1:35–36) What is interesting to me is the fact that after one afternoon with the Master Angler he became a successful fisher-of-men: "And the two disciples heard him speak, and they followed Jesus. Then Jesus turned, and saw them following, and saith unto them, What seek ye? They said unto him, Rabbi, (which is to say, being interpreted, Master,) where dwellest thou? He saith unto them, Come and see. They came and saw where he dwelt, and abode with him that day: for it was about the tenth hour. One of the two which heard John *speak*, and followed him, was Andrew, Simon Peter's brother. He first findeth his own brother Simon. . ." (John 1:37–41)

It was the well-known writer on fishing, Izaak Walton, that said: "As no man is born an artist so no man is born an angler!" I believe also that no man is born a 'fisher-of-men'; he must first be born again (John 3:3) and then with the tutorage of the Holy Spirit and only then can any man become a 'fisher-of-men'! A young Scottish fly fisherman (I have been an avid fly fisherman for fifty years) by the name of Thomas Boston wrote these lines in his diary on January 6, 1699: 'Follow me and I will make you fishers-of-men'. My soul cried out for the accomplishment of that in me, and I was very desirous to know how I might follow Christ, so as to be a fisher of men, and for my own instruction in that point I addressed myself to the consideration of it!" Boston, like Andrew, discovered that the best way to be a fisher-of-men was to follow the tactics of John taught to him. John pointed Andrew to Jesus and Andrew pointed his brother Simon to Jesus. That is what fishing for men is all about; simply pointing out Jesus to them and let the Spirit and Jesus do the rest! This is still the strategy of the Spirit to this day.

If Andrew's brother would eventually be called 'the Big Fisherman' because of all the people Peter point out Jesus too (nearly 3000 at Pentecost alone-Acts 2:41); then Andrew in my opinion ought to be called 'the little fisherman' because his fishing never involved a multitude but individuals. I have found it to be true that it is often the inexperienced and novice fishermen that catch the biggest fish. I remember once I had a favorite fishing hole and I finally persuaded my wife Coleen to go fishing with me there (she despised fishing), and sure enough she caught the biggest trout of the trip! We know of the great fisher-of-men in Church history like Moody, Spurgeon, and Graham, but we know little of the people that pointed them to Jesus. Such is the case when John's catch Andrew!

Andrew began his experience with Christ as a simple fisherman of fish on lake Galilee (Matthew 4:18). In his spare time he use to listen to the new prophet in town, John the Baptist, and John's message of the coming Messiah thrilled him. Finally the day came when John pointed Jesus out in the crowd and would watch as John baptized Jesus. It was then instead of following John Andrew with his friend John decided to follow Jesus. Where exactly John 1:35–39 fits into the day that Jesus walked the shores of Galilee and formally called Andrew and his brother Simon and their friends John and James (Matthew 4:18–22) to be Jesus' disciples is hard to figure, but whenever and wherever the stage was set to make Andrew a fisher of men. I believe Andrews experience gives us the pattern that we need to follow to this day. As I mentioned in our chapter on Peter (chapter 17), every time Andrew is the main character in a Gospel story he is bringing someone to Jesus, and these three stories give us the pattern laid down by Jesus in Acts 1:8: "But ye shall receive power, after that the Holy Ghost is come upon you: and ye shall be witnesses unto me both in Jerusalem, and in all Judaea, and in Samaria, and unto the uttermost part of the earth." Note if you will the three-fold pattern of Andrew's fishing:

1. **Andrew was a witness to his family**, "his Jerusalem" if you will (John 1:41–42). I have come to believe that these are the most difficult fishing holes in the world. Those who have fished in these seas know just how difficult they can be, yet Andrew found success almost immediately. Be brave; realize your first responsibility in witnessing is to those closest to you. Remember what Jesus told the demonic after his healing and desire to go with Jesus: "Return to thine own house, and shew how great things God hath done unto thee. And he went his way, and published throughout the whole city how great things Jesus had done unto him." (Luke 8:39) There is a reason that Jerusalem must be reached first!

2. **Andrew was a witness to his neighbor**, "his Judea and Samaria" if you will (John 6:8–9). This is often a very dark fishing hole because we don't know who is to be reached; we don't know who God is calling, but the lifeline must still be thrown ("throw out the lifeline across the dark waves" as the old hymn goes). We must keep fishing no matter what just like Andrew did that day in a crowd of over five thousand. How he found the lad we are not told, but he was the lad that would bless the crowd with his lunch, and you can't tell me this lad never got saved that day! Andrew led Simon to Christ and saw 3000 blessed, and Andrew lead the lad to Jesus and saw over 5000 blessed! Ours is not to consider the results that is up to God (Acts 2:47), we are to bring them one by one and won by one!

3. **Andrew was a witness abroad**, "his uttermost part of the world" if you will (John 12:20–22). I would have you note before we go on that all three stories are recorded in John's Gospel; remember John was there from the start and impressed with Andrew's fishing for men. These can be very dangerous fishing pools. Long before the more famous Gentiles were saved (Acts 8-Ehiopian eunuch

(chapter 8) and Acts 10-Cornelius (chapter 18) Andrew was already bring them to Jesus. "Till the Whole World Knows" was Andrew's motto and he believed Jesus original challenge to them: "...Fear not; from henceforth thou shalt catch men..." (Luke 5:10) We lose sight of Andrew after the Book of John and that is in my opinion because Andrew was a fly fisherman (one fish at a time) not a net fisherman!

# 22

## WON: PHILIP THE BETHSAIDAEAN
## BY: John 1:43

The day following Jesus would go forth into Galilee, and findeth Philip, and saith unto him, Follow me.

## ONE: JESUS

MOST OF US KNOW that according to Hebrews 12:2 Jesus is a 'finisher', but Jesus was also a 'finder'. Have we not seen in this book that Jesus found the Samaritan woman (chapter 4), the blind man outside Jericho (chapter 10), and the publican inside Jericho (chapter 19). And then Jesus found Philip as we see from our 'won by one' verse printed above, and then Philip found his friend Nathanael: "Philip findeth Nathanael, and saith unto him, We have found him, of whom Moses in the law, and the prophets, did write, Jesus of Nazareth, the son of Joseph." (John 1:45) The 'finder' makes 'finders'. I like Charles Spurgeon on this when he wrote in his Evening and Morning devotional, and I quote: "This case is an excellent pattern of all cases where spiritual life is vigorous. As soon as a man has found Christ, he begins to find others. I will not believe that thou hast tasted of the honey of the gospel if thou canst eat it all thyself. True grace puts an end to all spiritual monopoly. Philip first found his dear friend Nathanael, and then others. Relationship has a very strong demand upon our first individual efforts. Philip, thou doest well to begin with Nathanael, I doubt whether there are not some Christians giving away tracts at other people's houses who would do well to give away a tract at their own-whether there are not some engaged in works of usefulness abroad who are neglecting their special sphere of usefulness at home. You mayst or thou mayst not be called to evangelize the people in any particular locality, but certainly thou art called to see after thine own servants, thine own kinsfolk and acquaintance. Let thy religion begin at home. Many tradesmen export their best commodities-the Christian should not. He should have all his conversation everywhere of the best Saviour; but let him have a care to put forth the sweetest fruit of spiritual life and testimony with his own family and friends. When Philip went to find his friend Nathanael, he little imagined that Nathanael would also be called to be one of the chosen twelve. . .You may be very deficient in talent yourself, and yet you may be the means of drawing to Christ one who shall become eminent in grace and service. Ah! dear friend, you little know the possibilities which are in you. You may but speak a word to a child, and in that child there may be slumbering a noble heart which shall stir the Christian Church in years to come. Jesus found Philip and Philip found Nathanael. Go thou and do likewise!" Are you a finder yet?

"Now Philip was of Bethsaida, the city of Andrew and Peter." (John 1:44) In 2010 I had the privilege to visit Bethsaida on the banks of the Sea of Galilee. I found an empty place, an archeological site at best, and yet I was happy to visit the place where Jesus called so many of his special disciples from. Chances are that half (Peter, Andrew, James, John, Philip, and Nathanael) of the Apostles came from Bethsaida; not doubt childhood friends because Bethsaida was a small fishing village on the north shore of Galilee, but for us in this devotional on "Won by One' we are focusing in on the Finder and His finders. Did not Andrew find Simon (John 1:40-42) to get the pattern established? So why did Jesus chose these friends from Bethsaida to be his closet friends and entrust and instruct them in the establishment of the Church. I have done an extensive study on the Twelve Apostles and I have come to believe that each of them brought into the group a special ability and talent that when combined made them the unstoppable group they would eventually become, and I believe Philip was the practical one; a very orderly man, reasonable and logical. When questioned by his friend Nathanael to the truth concerning his claim that he had found the Messiah, Philip simply replied: "Come and See!" (John 1:46) When questioned by the Lord as to how the multitude was to be feed Philip had already figured out how much it would cost to feed them all (John 6:5-7). Philip was the type that was probably thinking as Peter stepped out of the boat to walk to Jesus: 'water is a liquid and not a solid, trying to walk on water is a foolish thing, you will sink'! But such men make great fishers-of-men because they are focused and straightforward!

You and Ihave meet people like Philip in our journey through this old world: prompt, predictable, pragmatic, methodical, mathematical, and mechanical, just to list a few adjectives that describe them. Yet those kinds of people are usually very nearsighted and a spiritual man with limited vision can be very dangerous in evangelism: "Where there is no vision people perish!" (Proverbs 29:18) Later in the Gospel story this nearsightedness comes out clearly in the case of Philip. When approached by a group of Greeks with ". . .we would see Jesus. . ." (John 12:21) Philip first needs to find Andrew to see what he should do. As we discovered in our last chapter, Andrew had the foresight, the farsightedness to know that eventually the Gentiles would get the Gospel as well as the Jews. Philip hadn't seen beyond Jesus command: ". . .Go not into the way of the Gentiles, and into *any* city of the Samaritans enter ye not; but go rather to the lost sheep of the house of Israel." (Matthew 10:5–6) Philips timing was off. Another story that verifies this insight into the character of Philip took place on the night of the Last Supper with his slowness to recognize the Father in Jesus: "Philip saith unto him, Lord, shew us the Father, and it sufficeth us. Jesus saith unto him, Have I been so long time with you, and yet hast thou not known me, Philip? he that hath seen me hath seen the Father; and how sayest thou *then*, Shew us the Father?" (John 14:8–9) Though Philip would start his discipleship with Jesus very nearsighted, Jesus would transform him like he did the other disciples into a farsighted Christian seeking the lost to the ends of the world. Won by one isn't wrong as we see with Philip and Nathanael, but we must never be content to stay the way we start. A teachable spirit will allow the Teacher to change you into the fisher-of-men He wants of you. I remember when I had a small town vision, but over our sixty plus years together the Lord God has opened my eyes to small towns in India as well.

When the Great Commission was give and carried out Philip was a part of that world-wide vision (Acts 1:13). Though his name isn't directly mentioned in the early history of the Church as described by Luke, he did his part to establish the Church at Jerusalem and extend the Church into Judea and Samaria and eventually expand the Church into the uttermost parts of the earth. This nearsighted disciple became the farsighted apostle and according to Polycrates, an early Church historian, was ". . .one of the great lights of Asia. . ." From finding Nathanael to finding nations, Philip was one of Jesus great students in his 'finding' course. One of the great plagues in the modern Church is described in these words by John to the Church of Laodicea: "Because thou sayest, I am rich, and increased with goods, and have need of nothing; and knowest not that thou art wretched, and miserable, and poor, **and blind**, and naked: I counsel thee. . .and anoint thine eyes with eyesalve, that thou mayest see." (Revelation 3:17–18) What kind of evangelistic sight do you have: nearsighted, farsighted, or just plain blind?

# 23

## WON: DIONYSIUS THE AREOPAGITE
## BY: Acts 17:34

Howbeit certain men clave unto him, and believed: among the which *was* Dionysius the Areopagite, and a woman named Damaris, and others with them.

## ONE: PAUL

WE KNOW NOTHING ABOUT Dionysius except he was a man from Athens who was Won by One because of Paul's famous message commonly titled" 'the unknown God' (Acts 17:23). It is only fitting that the Unknown God would have unknown followers!

Many times in Scripture we are told of individuals and their acts of faith, trust, bravery, and loyalty to God, but they remain unnamed. Many years ago I put together a series of devotional (fifty of them) under the title of "Unnamed but not Unknown": people like the Samaritan woman (see chapter 4), the Calvary thief (see chapter 16), the Ethiopian eunuch (see chapter 8), the Philippian jailer (see chapter 12), and the Capernaum centurion (see chapter 20) to name a few. A few years after that study I decided I needed to put together another devotional book on "Unknown but not Unnamed". Dionysius falls in that category and there are a multitude of names that fall into this group. Surely your reading of the Bible has uncovered individuals where only their name is given and you have asked yourself the question: "Who was that?" At least with Dionysius we know something about him, for he is numbered by Luke in his Acts of the Apostles of Paul's trophies from his stay in Athens, but there the story ends, or does it? As with all other unknowns or unnamed there is always something more to the story!

We know it didn't end there, but Biblically speaking it does end there. Perhaps, that is the importance of Dionysius being named? Perhaps, that is the importance of those long lists of names recorded both in the Old Testament and the New Testament (genealogies). I have just finished reading again the Book of Ezra, and in that short ten-chapter history much of the telling is given over to listing names, and we know nothing about these individuals but their names (Ezra 2:2–57, 7:1–5, 8:1–14, and 10:20–44) Who was Chelluh (Ezra 10:35), or Jeshaiah (Ezra 8:7) or Meraioth (Ezra 7:3) or Azgad (Ezra 2:12)? If you would like some practice pronouncing Biblical names that would illustrate my point dramatically read I Chronicles 1–9. I rest my case. Who are these unknown but not unnamed characters of the Bible; who was Dionysius?

I have come to believe (Romans 14:5) that Dionysius was singled out for honorable mention because he was the only Areopagite converted on Mars Hill (Acts 17:22). To be there, and to respond positively to a new philosophy, a new message, a new religion, a new God, and a new way of life made Dionysius unique indeed for his age and the age-old faith the Greeks believed in. Rare have been the individuals throughout history that have gone it alone, pioneering a new path, launching out in a new direction, but Dionysius did; Abraham-like wouldn't you say? Remember Abram lived in an era where nobody worshiped a single god. Even Abram started life believing in the 'gods' (Joshua 24:2), but like Dionysius he heard the voice of the true and living God and followed him. That was where Dionysius was when Paul showed up and saw all the gods on Mars Hill and the Greeks were so afraid they had missed one they decided to make an altar to 'the unknown god' and it was at that altar Paul told Dionysius about the Lord Jesus Christ. I believe this is another reason we can ponder the importance of Dionysius because he was the one Jesus was talking about when he told Thomas: "Jesus saith unto him, Thomas, because thou hast seen me, thou hast believed: blessed *are* they that have not seen, and *yet* have believed." (John 20:29) Dionysius was a forerunner of those who didn't see but believed and believed if nobody else would. Peter would write of Dionysius: "Whom having not seen, ye love; in whom, though now ye see *him* not, yet believing, ye rejoice with joy unspeakable and full of glory." (I Peter 1:8) And though they were unknown they were known of Christ and He used them in the shadows where nobody saw!

Dionysius was willing to depart from the common belief of his people and accept something totally enlightening. Perhaps, he had been searching for years for this unknown god, but after hearing Paul's sermon on Jesus and the resurrection (Acts 18:31–32) he was convinced where others weren't. I have used this story for years to tell of the three responses of those that hear a Gospel message: there are those that will mock and laugh, there are those that will say I want more information, and praise God there are those that will believe (Acts 17:34)! I love the phrase that Dionysius **'clave unto him'**. It took courage and conviction to do this in light of the reaction of the crowd and that same courage and conviction is needed today for to accept Christ today you will face what Dionysius faced and what could be said of Dionysius can be said of Damaris (the lady who responded like Dionysius and what do we know of her). When I think of the Damaris of the Church I think of ladies like Audrey Wetherel Johnson, the founder of the Bible Study Fellowship who at the age of 29 in 1936 went to China and there between 1942–1945 was interned by the Japanese and her weight dropped from 145 to 109 but through it all kept the faith, and if I had time I would speak of Corrie ten Boom and so many other woman who kept the faith despite its unpopularity! But also note there are also the unnamed and the unknown in our key verse as well!

For his acts of faith Dionysius was listed with the other great individuals of the infant Church who when they heard they believed: there was Lydia of Philippi (Acts 16:140 and Phebe of Cenchrea (Romans 16:1) and Priscilla of Corinth (Acts 18:2) and Dorus of Joppa (Acts 9:36). Dr. Elton Trueblood, the founder of Yokefellows International, once made this comment on these New Testament pioneers of the Church: "So important were these individuals in the infant Church, that we are driven to the conclusion that, without their assistance, survival would have not occurred. Unknowns were in the total ministry because all were needed. Otherwise survival was not possible!" And Dionysius was one and Damaris was one, named but unknown but without them would we be here today?

Dear reader, are you known only by your name? I know it is difficult to go it alone at times. It is hard to break the bonds of unbelief, but believe in Jesus as Dionysius did and become more than a face in a crowd. Become the believer of your family, your block, your community or your state. Be named among the faithful few that respond to the Gospel call and be numbered among the unknown but not unnamed in the Lamb's Book of Life in Heaven (Revelation 21:27). Just because you have been lost in this world you are not only named in heaven but you are known in heaven just like Dionysius was. Someday it will be said of you as Paul wrote to the Church in Corinth: "...as unknown, and yet well known..." (II Corinthians 6:9) Earthly books might be void of your spiritual conversion and exploits for Christ but the books of heaven will tell a different story. So like Paul let us win them one by one and tell them though they might not get famous here their conversion and exploits will be well known in heaven. Amen and Amen and Amen!

# 24

## WON: THE ALABASTER WOMAN
## BY: Luke 7:37–38

And, behold, a woman in the city, which was a sinner, when she knew that *Jesus* sat at meat in the Pharisee's house, brought an alabaster box of ointment, and stood at his feet behind *him* weeping, and began to wash his feet with tears, and did wipe *them* with the hairs of her head, and kissed his feet, and anointed *them* with the ointment.

## ONE: JESUS

I HAVE FOUND IN my long life as a Christian (I just turned 64 in my spiritual age, when I was born again and started a new life in Him) that I can relate more clearly to the unsung, unnamed, and little known heroes and heroines of the Bible than I can to the more famous and familiar characters of God's Hall of Fame recorded in Holy Writ. For the majority of us in the Christian Church our service for the Lord of lords and King of kings also goes unrecognized by the world and often by the Church. But that doesn't mean we should act any less faithfully, thoughtfully, or confidently. I believe it was for people like you and me, the least among us, the ordinary people, and the little person that the Scriptures are also filled with stories like the one shared above. Those unnamed shooting stars that suddenly appear and just a s quickly disappears from the pages of God's inspired Word. We should never forgets Paul's teaching on this: "All scripture *is* given by inspiration of God, and *is* profitable for doctrine, for reproof, for correction, for instruction in righteousness; that the man of God may be perfect, throughly furnished unto all good works." (II

Timothy 3:16–17) Note is says 'all', which includes the lady we are going to highlight and underline in this "Won by One' devotional. We can be challenged by these men and women, boys and girls, though we will have to wait until Heaven to know their names, yet their inspired exploits for God have become familiar to us. The one that I remind you of in this article is known for her sacrificial giving, act of devotion and extreme valor: the woman with the alabaster box!

As with the other chapters without names (see 4, 8, 12, 16, and 20- do you see the pattern I am sharing), I have given this woman a title. For years I have been under the false impression that the lady mentioned in this Gospel story was none other than Mary, the sister of Martha and Lazarus. This is an often misunderstood because of the similarities in the two stories. But I think you will conclude as I eventually did if you check Matthew 26:6, Mark 14:3 and John 12:2 that Mary copied this lady's actions, but she was not Mary. So though there are similarities and familiarities in the two tales, we are talking about a named individual and an unnamed individual, and it is this unnamed but not unknown individual that is the heroine in this 'won by one' chapter!

The first difference is that this story takes place in Capernaum (Luke 7:1, 37) while Mary's anointing took place in Bethany (John 12:1). If you know your Biblical geography: Capernaum is in Galilee and Bethany is just outside of Jerusalem. The second difference is that this story takes place in the home of a Pharisee (Luke 7:36) while Mary's deed took place in the home of Simon the leper (Matthew 26:6). For those who think that Simon the leper was a Pharisee (Luke 7:40) we know from that time that the Pharisees were very strict and no leper could have ever become a Pharisee. The third difference is that this story takes place early in the ministry of Jesus (compare context of Matthew 8:5–13 with Luke 7:1–10) while Mary's touching act was a pre-anointing of the Lord just before His death (Matthew 26:12). No! As Merrill Unger put it in his general information book on the Bible: "This woman was neither Mary of Bethany (John 12:1–8) nor Mary Magdalene. She was an unchaste woman, a prostitute, likely converted under John's or Jesus' ministry, who gave public evidence of her conversion and gratitude for her salvation!" About the only thing we can write about these two women is that their gifts were similar, their actions were similar, and one was named and the other unnamed!

During the debate of who this woman was, we often overlook and forget the marvelous lesson Jesus was trying to teach the Pharisee and his party. Perhaps, therein lies another reason why the Holy Spirit chose to leave this woman unnamed. For most of us we see the person instead of the problem, but with a nameless woman our attention turns away from the lady to the focus of her sin! Note these phrases in the story: "...a sinner...what manner of woman this is that toucheth Him: for she is a sinner...her sins which were many..." (Luke 7:37, 39, 47) One of the problems with our society today is we are just focusing on people with the neglect of their sin, and "For all have sinned, and come short of the glory of God." (Romans 3:23) We set our eyes on the well-dressed, the well-groomed in the three-piece suit or the beautiful dress; outwardly handsome, pretty yet inside are the ugliness and hideousness and wickedness of sin. No matter how innocent the outward appearance, inside: "The heart *is* deceitful above all *things*, and desperately wicked: who can know it?" (Jeremiah 17:9) Stories like this in the Bible that cut to the heart of the issue remind us that so should we. The depraved, Adamic nature is in that lovely baby girl, or that gorgeous, mature lady! Warning, however, that when we can see them as they are, we should never forget that no matter how much a sinner they are: they are forgivable. Most of us who see the sin and not the sinner's act react like Simon: "Now when the Pharisee which had bidden him saw *it*, he spake within himself, saying, This man, if he were a prophet, would have known who and what manner of woman *this is* that toucheth him: for she is a sinner." (Luke 7:39) For most of us we don't openly critical, pre-judge, or condemn, but under our breath we do all three. I think Jesus wants us to learn from this story not only to recognize sin, but that there is a remedy.

Jesus clearly rebuked Simon with a simple parable about two debtors (read carefully Luke 7:41–42). The principle and precept about to whom much is forgiven there is much love, but to whom little is forgiven there is little love is plainly and clearly taught not only in 'the alabaster woman' story but Jesus' classic parable. Compared to Simon the woman was as terrible sinner, yet compared to the sinner Simon was a terrible lover. How did Jesus discern that? Read Luke 7:44–46! It isn't enough for us to sing: "Oh, how I love Jesus." Love is like faith: "Even so faith, if it hath not works, is dead, being alone. Yea, a man may say, Thou hast faith, and I have works: shew me thy faith without thy works, and I will shew thee my faith by my works... But wilt thou know, O vain man, that faith without works is dead?" (James 2:17–18, 20) Even so love without action is dead, so the very act of this woman of pouring the alabaster box of ointment over Jesus was her way of saying thank you, an act of gratitude and thanksgiving for what I believe was her salvation. What would make her do that on a whim, or for no reason. I believe there was a reason and that reason was her conversion and she found a very public way of confessing: "Whosoever therefore shall confess me before men, him will I confess also before my Father which is in heaven." (Matthew 10:32). And so should we!

So this is our purpose in fishing for men; to see beyond the faults of the unnamed and to find a way to bring them to Christ: to see beyond their faults to see their eternal need!

# 25

## WON: HAGAR THE EGYPTIAN
## BY: Genesis 16:13

And she called the name of the LORD that spake unto her, Thou God seest me: for she said, Have I also here looked after him that seeth me?

## ONE: GOD

HAVE YOU EVER WONDERED how Hagar got into the family of Abram? My opinion is this: "And there was a famine in the land: and Abram went down into Egypt to sojourn there; for the famine *was* grievous in the land. . . And he entreated Abram well for her sake: and he had sheep, and oxen, and he asses, and menservants, and **maidservants**, and she asses, and camels." (Genesis 12:10, 16) I have come to believe that Hagar was one of those 'maidservants' Pharaoh gave Abram to buy him off over the Sarai affair? Remember this all happened when Abram (still working on his trust of God) didn't trust God during a time of famine and sought a safer place in Egypt, but also he couldn't trust God with his beautiful wife, so he lied and had Sarai lie resulting in Hagar coming into their family as Sarah's maid because despite Abram and Sarai' lack of faith He was still determined to use them. However, the Hagar (Genesis 16:1) story is a reminder that sometimes when you go on your own something happens that will alter your future story!

About ten years later: ". . .Abram *was* seventy and five years old when he departed out of Haran. . . And Abram *was* fourscore and six years old, when Hagar bare Ishmael to Abram." (Genesis 12:4, 16:16) when God had not yet (remember not yet) fulfilled His promise (Genesis

15:4) of a son for Abram and Sarai, they both agreed that Hagar might be the human answer to God's promise? How often do we try to help God? I know I have instead of waiting patiently for Him to do what only He can do. When impatience sets in; it had been ten years hadn't it? Impatience leads us to do some stupid things, but we rationalize it by saying we are just helping God out. God doesn't need our help! It started with this statement by Sarai: "And Sarai said unto Abram, Behold now, the LORD hath restrained me from bearing: I pray thee, go in unto my maid; it may be that I may obtain children by her. And Abram hearkened to the voice of Sarai." (Genesis 16:2) For me, the real tragedy is that Abram went along with his wife's counsel. What Abram need to learn in his faith, as we need to learn, and that is God is never too fast or too slow when it comes to His promises. God understands our impatience; He understands our attitude about important things, but He also likes to test us (Abram's tests aren't over-read Genesis 22); the only way our faith will grow and mature. Abram's and Sarai plan was destined to backfire on them and Hagar, but God had His eye on Hagar!

The result of this sin was only more sin. First, the pregnancy of Hagar resulted in jealousy by Sarai (Genesis 16:4). Then the harshness on Hagar by Sarai resulted in Hagar running away. I really like F. B. Meyer on this event. He wrote in a book called: "Great Verses Through the Bible", and I quote: "Poor Hagar! No wonder that she fled. Her proud Arab independence and the sense of coming motherhood made her rebel against Sarah's hard dealings. We have often mediated flight. If we have not actually fled from intolerable conditions. Of course, when God opens the door out of a dungeon we need not hesitate, as Peter did, to rise and follow. But this is very different to flight from the post of duty!" Yet it was in this flight Hagar would really find the God that I believe Abram and probably Sarai had been telling her about since Egypt. Romans 8:28: "And we know that all things work together for good to them that love God, to them who are the called according to *his* purpose;" this verse in highlighted and underlined in Hagar.

What took place in that desert setting was an encounter with Jehovah God and a fearful maid? As Philip found the Ethiopian eunuch near Gaza (Acts 8), so God found Hagar: "And the angel of the LORD found her by a fountain of water in the wilderness, by the fountain in the way to Shur." (Genesis 16:7) What a pattern we have discovered as we have traced these "Won by One" characters through the Bible. A seeking God will find a seeking sinner anywhere, even a wandering one, or a fleeing one. God knew where Hagar was, and He had a purpose for her, but often He makes a hard demand. For the rich young ruler it was to sell all he had (Matthew 19:16-22), but for Hagar it was: "And the angel of the LORD said unto her, Return to thy mistress, and submit thyself under her hands." (Genesis 16:9) Again I like what F. B. Meyer wrote about this conversion: "Return and submit. We are apt to suppose that we shall get rest and peace elsewhere. It is not so, however. Nowhere else shall we find the path of less rugged, or the pillow less hard. To evade the yoke will not give us heart ease. The Master's advice is that we shall take His yoke (Matthew 11:28-30), and bear it as He did; remain where God has put us, till He show us another place (Genesis 21); and bear what He ordains and permits, even though it comes through the means of others. We cannot patiently submit to our lot unless we believe that what God permits is as much His will as what He appoints. Behind Sarah's hard dealing we must behold his permissive providence. Through all the discipline of life we must believe that God has a purpose of unfailing love and wisdom. Then our submission is not stoicism, but loving acquiescence in our Father's will!" And I have come to the persuasion that this was the case for Hagar, and her doing what God told her to do, despite how hard it was; tells me that she had come to trust the God of Abram and Sarai. Her name is not mentioned by James, but I believe he could have: "Yea, a man may say, Thou hast faith, and I have works: shew me thy faith without thy works, and I will shew thee my faith by my works." (James 2:18) Often overlooked!

Despite this multitude of sins in this story, God again showed mercy and grace both to Hagar and Sarai. Hagar would return at God's command, but we all knew it wouldn't be long before the two women would be at odds again. There was a reason God ordained one man for one woman. Just like anything that has two heads it is not only a monstrosity but a recipe for disaster. The eventual birth of Ishmael began a clock ticking that would within 14 years result in another departure by Hagar from the campsite of Abraham and Sarah, and Hagar's second encounter with God: "And she went, and sat her down over against *him* a good way off, as it were a bowshot: for she said, Let me not see the death of the child. And she sat over against *him*, and lift up her voice, and wept. And God heard the voice of the lad; and the angel of God called to Hagar out of heaven, and said unto her, What aileth thee, Hagar? fear not; for God hath heard the voice of the lad where he *is*." (Genesis 21:16-17) For me, this is a verification of what took place during that first desert encounter.

When Hagar was in trouble she turned to the Lord and the Lord hear her, as one of his children. Rejected by Abraham and Sarah, accepted by their God, and so it will be for those that put their trust in Jesus Christ as their Saviour. There will come times when we will have to let go of family or friends, but God will never let us go. Why Hagar? Only God knows, and it might be as simple as Acts 10:35 again. God needed an Egyptian around His throne one day and He found in Hagar's heart what He wanted!

# 26

## WON: NATHANAEL THE SKEPIC
## BY: John 1:49

Nathanael answered and saith unto him, Rabbi, thou art the Son of God; thou art the King of Israel.

## ONE: PHILIP

For me, one of the most skeptical questions ever asked in the Bible has to be Nathanael's classic: "Can there any good thing come out of Nazareth?" (John 1:46) Philip had just meet the Lord, and like Andrew was eager to share his new find with a close friend. I believe Philip and Nathanael were best friends, so it would be logical for Philip to go to Nathanael and say: "Philip findeth Nathanael, and saith unto him, We have found him, of whom Moses in the law, and the prophets, did write, Jesus of Nazareth, the son of Joseph." (John 1:45) Philip had been persuaded, but Nathanael like his generation was skeptical. I have come to believe that there is nothing wrong with a sincere question even if it is a skeptical one. I have meet many skeptic, for are we not living in a skeptical age? "Knowing this first, that there shall come in the last days scoffers, walking after their own lusts, and saying, Where is the promise of his coming? For since the fathers fell asleep, all things continue as *they were* from the beginning of the creation." (II Peter 3:3-4) Instead of arguing with Nathanael Philip simply said: "Come and See!" (John 1:46) By now you must know that one of my favorite writers is the southern revivalist Vance Havner. I love this by Vance on Philip and Nathanael: "Philip did not let Nathanael sidetrack him into a discussion of whether or not any good thing could come out of Nazareth. That was irrelevant and Philip was no authority on the matter. After all, the best way to settle that question, as well as all others, was 'come and see for yourself.' Jesus was just out of Nazareth, and Nathanael could soon find out the answer for his query. The Devil likes to sidetrack us from the real issue. The woman at Jacob's well raised secondary matters until the Lord brought her to face her sins and Himself as the Messiah. Do not let people dodge the real issue by raising a lot of unimportant questions. Tell them to come to Christ and see for themselves. He is in Himself the answer to all our problems. Whatever you may not understand, whatever puzzles you, do not try to solve such things one by one. Come to Him and He will dispel your doubts and you will say with Nathanael, 'Thou art the Son of God'!" To which I say Amen and Amen!

Nathanael's sincerity was also revealed in Jesus' first words to him: "Jesus saw Nathanael coming to him, and saith of him, Behold an Israelite indeed, *in whom is no guile!*" (John 1:47) What a testimony for an unsaved man. I believe there are some very good sinner out there, for I have meet a few of them in my life. As a matter of fact, I have meet a few sinner that put many Christians I know to shame. Why was this statement by Christ so profound? Peter would say this about the Christ: "Who did no sin, **neither was guile found in his mouth**." (I Peter 2:22) The thought in both verses means 'no craftiness, no deceit'. Jesus was saying Nathanael was an honest and a trustworthy man, just like Him. Nathanael was already Christ-like before he was a Christian. Paul would write: "For our exhortation *was* not of deceit, nor of uncleanness, **nor in guile!**"

(I Thessalonians 2:3) Nathanael was no hypocrite, but Nathanael was still no Christian. Just because you are morally right and live a good life remember all our good is not good enough for God (Isaiah 64:6), but I believe this observation of Jesus about Nathanael tells us that Nathanael was a genuine skeptic, and I have found that you can get a lot further with a genuine, sincere skeptic than you can with a hypocritical saint! But Nathanael was still like all good, honest, sincere people, he still needed a Savour, but his friend Philip had brought him to the right Man, for in Jesus of Nazareth he would find the Saviour.

When Nathanael finally did hear the Christ, he makes one of the clearest confessions of faith in the Bible: "Rabbi, thou art the Son of God; thou art the King of Israel!" When reality finally sunk into Nathanael's heart his skepticism become salvation; his concern become conversion, and his doubts lead to discipleship. I believe Nathanael's confession equals that of Peter's confession: "And Simon Peter answered and said, Thou art the Christ, the Son of the living God." (Matthew 16:16) And Thomas' later confession: "And Thomas answered and said unto him, My Lord and my God." (John 20:28) That moment salvation came to the skeptic and from that moment onward Nathanael saw Jesus as his Lord and Governor; all because he came to see for himself what his friend Philip had told him about this Jesus of Nazareth. He questioned at first where Jesus was from, but once he meet Jesus where he was from no longer mattered. And because Nathanael saw in Jesus the Christ, Jesus told him she would see much more: "Jesus answered and said unto him, Because I said unto thee, I saw thee under the fig tree, believest thou? thou shalt see greater things than these. And he saith unto him, Verily, verily, I say unto you, Hereafter ye shall see heaven open, and the angels of God ascending and descending upon the Son of man." (John 1:50-51) Charles Spurgeon, the great English pastor, writes this on Jesus statement to Nathanael in his book "Evening and Morning", and I quote: "Yes, to our faith this sight is plain even at this day. We do see heaven opened. Jesus Himself has opened that kingdom to all believers. We gaze into the place of mystery and glory, for He has revealed it to us. We shall enter it soon, for He is the Way. Now we see the explanation of Jacob's ladder. Between heaven and earth, there is a holy commerce; prayer ascends and answers come down by the way of Jesus, the Mediator. We see this ladder when we see our Lord. In Him a stairway of light now furnisher a clear passage to the throne of the most high. Let us use it, and send up by it the messengers of our prayers. We shall live the angelic life ourselves if we run up to heaven in intercession, and lay hold upon the blessings of the covenant, and then descend again to scatter those gifts among the sons of men. This choice sight which Jacob only saw in a dream will turn into a bright reality. This very day we will be up and down the ladder each hour, climbing in communion, and coming down in labor to save our fellowmen. This is thy promise, O Lord Jesus; let us joyfully see it fulfilled." Again I simply say Amen and Amen!

Perhaps, you know a searching skeptic? You can't tell me that Philip didn't already know probably what Nathanael's reply to him would be; friends know friends. That is why I believe Philip didn't argue with his friend, but simply took him to Jesus. Maybe, that is the reason you are reading this today; for yourself or another. Follow Philip's lead, and then follow Jesus' lead. If you are the Philip then become a member of the 'won by one' club. If you are the Nathanael then become a member of the 'one by won' fraternity! All your need is Jesus and all your friend needs is Jesus, so you and they must make that rendezvous soon than later, before it is too late (Isaiah 55:6). Remember, our words will return void, but we have a promise that His words won't: "So shall my word be that goeth forth out of my mouth: it shall not return unto me void, but it shall accomplish that which I please, and it shall prosper *in the thing* whereto I sent it." (Isaiah 55:11) Remember, Jesus does want to use you to bring your friend to Himself; go get him today!

# 27

**WON**: EPAENETUS THE ACHAEAN
**BY**: Romans 16:5

Likewise *greet* the church that is in their house. Salute my wellbeloved Epaenetus, who is the firstfruits of Achaia unto Christ.

**ONE**: PAUL

THERE IS SOMETHING ABOUT being the first. It has been the goal of many in this world to be first at something, or doing something, or going somewhere; to be the first to scale a mountain like Hillary, or to across an ocean like Lindbergh, or step on the moon like Armstrong. Most of those that do such things are unknown, but when they accomplish their first they were in the spotlight and still are known to this day for that first. I have come to believe in my study of the Holy Bible that there is an importance to the 'first' of something, or someone. Theologically this doctrine has become known as 'the principle of first mention'. This concept has been defined in this manner: "That principle by which God indicates in the first mention of a subject the truth with which that subject stands connected in the mind of God!" To illustrate this precept and to continue our search through the Scriptures for our 'won by one' individuals I would have you turn your attention to the verse I have printed for you above. First, this is the one and only time that the man Epaenetus is mentioned in the Bible; a first and a last. Second, Epaenetus' only call to Biblical fame is the fact that he was Paul's first convert in the region of Achaia. Despite the fifty-five years that has passed I still remember fondly my firstfruits in witnessing. Mary Huff was her name and she was a resident of a nursing home in Athens, Georgia. I also remember clearly my firstfruits in my very first church ministry in Pembroke, New Hampshire. Her name was Jane Call, and she lived next door to the small community center we were renting at the time to have our services. I recall vividly the campfire that Claude Levick came to a saving knowledge of Jesus Christ, my firstfruit in Christian camping ministries. I was with a Boy's Brigade group in northern Quebec, Canada when the conversion took place. In the back of a record book of my ministries I have a list of all the 'won by one' firsts I have experienced in a variety of spiritual works, so with the help of Epaenetus and Paul let me highlight and underlines this precept of first mention in relationship to bringing someone to the saving knowledge of Jesus.

Dr. A. T. Pierson writes: "This is a law we have long since noted, and have never yet found it to fail. The first occurrence of a word, expression, or utterance is a key to its subsequent meaning, or it will be a guide to ascertaining the essential truth connected to it!" Let us take this description and apply it to the mention of Epaenetus and firstfruits. The Apostle Paul often connected 'fruits; to conversions: "Now I would not have you ignorant, brethren, that oftentimes I purposed to come unto you, (but was let hitherto,) *that I might have some fruit among you also*, even as among other Gentiles." (Romans 1:13) Paul was certainly speaking about evangelistic fruit in this verse in relationship to the Gentiles in Rome. So when Paul ends his letter to the Romans with a mention of Epaenetus **(which means praise)** his first convert in Achaia he was but illustrating the desire he spoke of at the beginning of the epistle. What should be our first reaction to the saving of a soul? I say 'praise'! "Likewise, I say unto you, there is joy (praise) in the presence of the angels of God over one sinner that repenteth." (Luke 15:10) Check it our carefully that in each of the three stories that Jesus tells about something lost being found the common denominator is 'rejoicing', a praise party if you will over the results. For the lost sheep (Luke 15:6), for the lost silver (Luke 15:9), and for the lost son (Luke 15:24). When was the last time we had a praise service for the fruits of a Gospel meeting, or a Church service, or a convert at a youth camp? We party over about every other thing!

John Newton, the author of Amazing Grace, also wrote this about our principle: "I find in Scripture this principle of interpretation which I believe, if conscientiously adopted, will serve as an unfailing guide to what was in the mind of God. This is the keystone of the whole matter." If this be true then what else does the mention of Paul leading Epaenetus to Christ tell us? For me, it means that Epaenetus was just the first of many.

Only Jesus Christ is both the first and the last. (Revelation 1:8, 11) How many have followed Charles Lindbergh across the Atlantic in a plane; even I have many times! How many have followed Edmund Hillary up the slopes of Mount Everest, and Neil Armstrong is not the only man to step foot on the moon! If you check the mention of Achaia you will discover that Epaenetus was only one of many that got saved during Paul's tour of Achaia (I Corinthians 16:15–16). Was Epaenetus a member of the Stephanus family? I believe he was. Stephanus was probably the father and Epaenetus the son? But whether that family or another; Epaenetus was still the first to believe in the area of Achaia. A look at Luke's history of the mission trips of Paul will show that Lydia of Thyatira was the firstfruits of Europe, but she was not the last, for the Philippian jailer and his family quickly followed (Acts 16). This concept can be seen throughout the life of Paul, for wherever he went, whatever town he entered he had a firstfruit. Arthus Taylor was my firstfruit of my Westfield (my second church) ministry. Lee Belyea was my firstfruit of my hospital ministries. Ida Metcalfe was my firstfruits of my Eastport (my third church) ministry. Cris Plourde was my firstfruit of my Ellsworth (my last church) ministry. Julie Fulton was the firstfruit of my 38 year AWANA (youth ministry) work. Cris Roy was my firstfruit of a 25 year ministry at Hampton Christian Camp in New Brunswick, Canada. Kim Bakeman was my firstfruit of my writing ministry after reading one of my weekly articles to the people of the Emmanuel Baptist Church. LillyKully was my firstfruit of my India ministry that now includes seven trips to the subcontinent. As I write this book I have just returned from the State of Chhattisgarh in central India were on March 8, 2022 after the dedication service for the new Makdi Church sanctuary Tara and Joice Nag came up to me telling me that they had received Christ during my message. Firstfruits are only the beginning and whether Christian camping, short-term mission's trips there will always be firsts, but I believe never lasts! I would challenge you to check this doctrine out through your own experience or through the experience of others and you will find it is true!

Are you the firstfruit of your family? Take heart dear saint by the precept of first mention. Live the life before your family and friends constantly and daily and it won't be long before the firstfruit will multiply into more fruit (John 15:2) and then much fruit (John 15:5, 8). I believe these are the precepts that Jesus added to the concept we have been sharing. How many missionary stories I have read where the missionary labors for year after year to see no fruit, and then when the first finally comes that convert isn't the last. I found this to be true in my own life as the years have passed the firsts where followed by the seconds and the thirds and so on. Today let us press on by the encouragement that firstfruits are only the beginning of the harvest. "Of his own will begat he us with the word of truth, that we should be a kind of firstfruits of his creatures." (James 1:18) Firstfruits always lead to other fruit. Amen and Amen and Amen.

# 28

## WON: THE PRODIGAL SON
## BY: Luke 15:18

I will arise and go to my father, and will say unto him, Father,
I have sinned against heaven, and before thee.

## ONE: THE PRODIGAL'S FATHER

PERHAPS, ONE OF THE greatest and best known stories Jesus ever told was the parable of the prodigal son. I have come to believe (Romans 14:5) that it is a parable and not a true story, but it certainly has all the characteristics that it could be a true story. Must people see the tale as being a classic illustration of ruin to reconciliation, sinner to salvation? All the key ingredients are in the well-beloved story. Self-well to selfishness to separation resulted in the prodigal leaving the father's house. Then success to sensuality to starvation resulting in the prodigal remembering the father's house. As the old preacher used to say: "He went to the dogs and ended up eating with the hogs!" But in that lowly estate conviction gave way to confession which in turn resulted in contrition which manifested itself in conversion which in turn sent the prodigal back to the father's house. Over the years, I have noticed that so many look at the prodigal to the neglect of the prodigal's father, in my opinion, the real hero of the story! A few years back I committed myself to a period of time in which I focused my attention on this 21-verse story. A simple story, a short story but a story filled with precepts and concepts for dealing with a prodigal. I had one in my son Scott and I wanted to learn how to deal with him. I will leave all I learned, maybe for a book, yes, I think you could write a book on this story, for the purpose of this book: 'won by one'. The prodigal is certainly the 'won', and the father is the 'one'. Our topic will be the importance of the parent to the salvation of a child!

Maybe today, you are in the sandals of this father? Are you the parent of a prodigal? Do you have a runaway son, a rebellious daughter? Then these thoughts are for you, and I understand by experience exactly what you are going through. Have you ever noticed that Jesus shared this parable for you and me, and we both are given how to handle our prodigal and what to do when he returns? I have come to believe that if we follow the precepts of handling our prodigal, we one day will get him back; like I did! Three principles stand out to me in this area in the story: 1) a prodigal will not be allowed to ruin the home (Luke 15:12); 2) a prodigal will not be run after even if he gets into trouble (Luke 15:14), and 3) a prodigal son will only be received home after he has come to himself (Luke 15:17).We know what the prodigal was doing when he was away (Luke 15:13, 30), but have you ever noticed what the prodigal's father was doing?

I have come to this insight, but remember this is only my observations according to the text. First, I believe the father hadn't lost his love for the son nor "And be ye kind one to another, tenderhearted, forgiving one another, even as God for Christ's sake hath forgiven you." (Ephesians 4:32) Though the son didn't know it, the father was waiting with forgiveness, love, and kindness-"but when he was yet a great way off"! (Luke 15:20) For me, that is ANTICIPATION. The question isn't will he return, but are you ready for him to return. I have counseled many a parent with a prodigal and they are still hurt, embarrassed, and angry with their prodigal. Yet if you can forgive your prodigal, then the way is clear for their return. Second, I noticed an EXPECTATION-'and his father saw him'! (Luke 15:20) You don't see unless you are looking. There are many parents who aren't even looking. It seems this father was keeping a vigil. He wasn't in the field or no vacation; he was on the porch looking down the road and when the prodigal turned the corner for home the father saw him. It doesn't mention prayer but I believe many a supplication had gone up for the son from the lips of the father, and he was determined when the son knocked on the door he would be waiting to welcome him home; not the brother, not the servants, but himself. This might be considered undeserved kindness, but a divine kindness (Jonah 4:2) and that is why we see the Father in this father, and his reaction to each and every one of us when we turn to Him.

This father read nothing into the return of this son other than he had returned, but a third characteristic that is needed "and had compassion"! (Luke 15:20) COMPASSION is the key ingredient in this story. The father never questioned the son's motives, for he wouldn't even listen to his confession. Can you imagine what the prodigal looked like? Shoeless, what cloths he had tattered and torn, dirty, and smelling of pigs. Yet the father was moved with compassion; like Jesus (Matthew 9:36-Luke 13:34). I have come to believe that compassion is the virtue that stays at home when you hear that your son is sleeping with the pigs, but you are moved to run to him with a hug when he has come to himself and returns home. You can't tell me that this wealthy father didn't have the means to know where his son was and in what state he was in? Just like our heavenly Father knows all the troths we feed at! The prodigal was not ready for a hug in the far country, but a hug was waiting for him when he got back to the father's country! And then there was CONSOLATION-"and ran, and fell on his neck"! (Luke 15:20) There was no waiting on his son when he saw his son, but a quick run to meet him and a hug (fell on his neck) and what that hug must have meant to the son. Have you hugged your kid today? Don't wait until they return from a prodigal trip, for I am convinced many a would-be prodigal can be changed before they leave by a few extra hugs a day!

Finally, there is AFFECTION here: "and kissed him"! (Luke 15:20) This story is dominated by the father's love, not the brother's love, but the affection of the father for the prodigal son; this kind of love: "But God commendeth his love toward us, in that, while we were yet sinners, Christ died for us." (Romans 5:8) The reason the father wouldn't even entertain the son's confession is that he already saw the change. I feel the only place was in the face, for the father knows his sons. Yes, all that the father did was motivated by love: "And above all things have fervent charity among yourselves: for charity shall cover the multitude of sins." (I Peter 4:8) If one reads the story carefully one will recognize that this wasn't an ordinary parental love, for these actions of the father could only be seen as divine love; for only God's love ("Charity suffereth long, *and* is kind; charity envieth not; charity vaunteth not itself, is not puffed up, doth not behave itself unseemly, seeketh not her own, is not easily provoked, thinketh no evil; rejoiceth not in iniquity, but rejoiceth in the truth; beareth all things, believeth all things, hopeth all things, endureth all things. Charity never faileth..." (I Corinthians 13:4–8) can heal the wounds caused by a prodigal, heal the hurts caused by the prodigal, and heal the regret of the son.

To my three precepts about what to do with a prodigal I added these two precepts if the prodigal comes back: 4) A prodigal will be received with forgiveness when he returns, and 5) a prodigal's prodigy will be remembered no more! The brother (Luke 15:25–32) didn't have this attitude, but the father (I John 4:8) did.

Today, why don't you try godly love in dealing with your prodigal that is either living at home, or away from home? It could be your last chance in getting your prodigal back!

# 29

## WON: RAHAB THE AMORITE
## BY: Hebrews 11:31

By faith the harlot Rahab perished not with them that believed not, when she had received the spies with peace.

## ONE: GOD

WHEN PAUL MADE HIS list of the famous faithful from the Old Testament; his list contained all Jewish names except one: Rahab the harlot. Rahab was the only Gentile name, but Rahab wasn't the only Gentile, what of Ruth the Moabite (see chapter 15), or Eliezer the Syrian (see chapter 9) or Ebedmelech the Ethiopian (see chapter 11)? But in Paul's eyes only Rahab came up to the standard of his list. Also interestingly about the Amorite is the fact that five of the seven times her name appears in the Bible the phrase 'the harlot' is attached to her name. Most scholars feel she wasn't a harlot when she appears first on the pages of Scriptures, but simply a title of her former occupation. Yet the stigma stuck much like Simon the leper (Matthew 26:5) though again most believe he had been cured of leprosy by the time he comes into the Biblical text. The change of all of us is clearly described by Paul in his letter to the Corinthians: "Know ye not that the unrighteous shall not inherit the kingdom of God? Be not deceived: neither fornicators, nor idolaters, nor adulterers, nor effeminate, nor abusers of themselves with mankind, nor thieves, nor covetous, nor drunkards, nor revilers, nor extortioners, shall inherit the kingdom of God. And such were some of you: but ye are washed, but ye are sanctified, but ye are justified in the name of the Lord Jesus, and by the Spirit of our

God." (I Corinthians 6:9–11) Rahab the harlot would have been lost but for the grace of God!

If there was an individual who never should have gotten saved it has to be Rahab and her family! Rahab lived in the wicked city of Jericho (Genesis 15:16); an Amorite, a cursed people by God (Deuteronomy 7:1). Rahab was like the woman at the well, an immoral, sensual lady whose life had been the gutters of Jericho for most of her life. Besides being a fornicator and an idolater, she lived in a city under divine judgment just like Sodom. Jericho stood in the path of God's divine judgment and Rahab was in the middle of that road. That is why the divine precept invoked by Abraham was true in his day and still true in Rahab's day: "Wilt thou also destroy the righteous with the wicked?" (Genesis 18:23). Rahab's story tells me that before God could wipe out Jericho He had to somehow save, or protect Rahab through that destruction! For we know by the rest of the story that like righteous Lot (II Peter 2:7-8) Rahab had to be protected: "The Lord knoweth how to deliver the godly out of temptations, and to reserve the unjust unto the day of judgment to be punished." (II Peter 2:9) When Rahab became a believer we aren't told, but we are told that God "...knoweth them that are his..." (II Timothy 2:19) and before Jericho could be destroyed Rahab had to be cared for. So it is my opinion that the two spies (Joshua 2:9, 11) that went into Jericho to check out the defenses for Joshua went into Jericho to find Rahab and protect her, and that is exactly what happened.

I have come to believe that Rahab came to the Lord through hearing about the Lord, for she says this in her own testimony: "For we have heard how the LORD dried up the water of the Red sea for you, when ye came out of Egypt; and what ye did unto the two kings of the Amorites, that *were* on the other side Jordan, Sihon and Og, whom ye utterly destroyed. And as soon as we had heard *these things*, our hearts did melt, neither did there remain any more courage in any man, because of you: for the LORD your God, he *is* God in heaven above, and in earth beneath." (Joshua 2:10-11) Paul teaches: "So then faith *cometh* by hearing, and hearing by the word of God." (Romans 10:17) James would note this about Rahab: "Likewise also was not Rahab the harlot justified by works, when she had received the messengers, and had sent *them* out another way? For as the body without the spirit is dead, so faith without works is dead also." (James 2:25-26) For me, this is the Old Testament story of amazing grace (I Peter 5:10). Her step of faith and her service of faith saved herself and her family (Joshua 6:25). The harlot become the heroine not only to her family but to the entire nation of Israel, for she would eventually marry into the tribe of Judah and become the great, and add a few more greats, grandmother of David (Ruth 4:20–25) and be listed in the Messianic Line of the Christ (Matthew 1:5)!

Rahab starts her testimony with these words: "And she said unto the men, I know that the LORD hath given you the land, and that your terror is fallen upon us, and that all the inhabitants of the land faint because of you." (Joshua 2:9) How was Rahab converted? How did Rahab believe before she meet her first Jew? Rahab had already known the LORD before the two spies knocked on her door; who was the evangelist here? There can be only one answer: the Lord Himself. (check out chapter 1 and 25) I know I have printed these verses numerous times through this book, but it begs repeating again in the Rahab 'won by one' story: "...Of a truth I perceive that God is no respecter of persons: but in every nation he that feareth him, and worketh righteousness, is accepted with him." (Acts 34–35) Granted, there were more people in Jericho than Rahab (Joshua 6:23) who got saved, but I am convinced that Rahab was God's firstfruits in Jericho just like the woman at the well was Jesus' firstfruit in Samaria and as Lydia lead her family to the Lord and the Philippian jailer lead his family to the Lord (Acts 16), so did Rahab lead her family.

So what does this teach us about evangelism in the Old Testament? For me, it teaches that God used the events of His power to be spread by the travelling merchants of the day. How else would Rahab have heard of the events of Egypt and the Red Sea? The events from the other side of the Jordan and the Amorites on the east bank were more local, but still someone had to tell them, pass them on. Those somebodies probably were not believers themselves, but the news was enough to convince Rahab in the Lord. I have often wondered as I have read the Old Testament accounts how many more Rahab's and Ruth's were there; those that didn't figure into God Messianic plan, but still came as Rahab did to a belief in the true and living God? Whichever may be the case, the news of the power of God was enough for Rahab, and her heart was turned to believe in God and when the first opportunity came to serve God she did it even to the peril of her own life! I have come to believe that the same faith (Hebrews 11:31) that saved Rahab had saved Abraham before her: "And he believed in the LORD; and he counted it to him for righteousness." (Genesis 15:6) The unrighteous Rahab became the righteous Rahab. The unjustifiable resident of Jericho became the justified believer of Israel. From a wicked member of the Amorite race to a royal member of the Messianic line of Jesus Christ.

Are you living today with a sorted past? We can't change the past, but like Rahab we certainly can change the outcome of our lives if we will simply by faith put our hope and trust in God, and in particular His Son Jesus. Are you a sinner without an evangelist, without a witness in your town or family? Somebody might have failed to tell you about God as a child, but simply look and listen for God is still at work, for He is still in the business of taking sorted pasts and turning them into spectacular futures just like Rahab!

# 30

## WON: SAUL THE BENJAMITE
## BY: Acts 9:6

And he trembling and astonished said, Lord, what wilt thou have me to do? And the Lord *said* unto him, Arise, and go into the city, and it shall be told thee what thou must do.

## ONE: JESUS

I HAVE COME TO believe the greatest turnaround in history must be the story of the conversion of Saul the Benjamite (Philippians 3:5). Saul's story would be the equitant of General Robert E. Lee switching side on the middle day of the great battle at Gettysburg! Saul in one day switched from being the head of the opposition against the new Church to one day being the head of that Church. Saul, later called Paul, began his Biblical career by holding the garments of those that stoned the Church's first martyr (Acts 7:58). But Saul was more than a witness: "**And Saul was consenting unto his death.** And at that time there was a great persecution against the church which was at Jerusalem; and they were all scattered abroad throughout the regions of Judaea and Samaria, except the apostles." (Acts 8:1) Later in Saul's own testimony he wrote this: "Concerning zeal, persecuting the church. . ." (Philippians 3:6) When the great persecutions of the Church began it was Saul that struck the first, vicious blows! Luke would describe those blows this way: "As for Saul, he made havock of the church, entering into every house, and haling men and women committed *them* to prison." (Acts 8:3) Then Luke would add: "And Saul, yet breathing out threatenings and slaughter against the disciples of the Lord, went unto the high priest." (Acts 9:1) In the early days of the first major persecution Saul would hound and harass and hunt down every Christian he could find in Jerusalem, and when he had scattered the Church, he would chase them afar, even as far as Damascus (Acts 9:2). Again, in another part of Saul's testimony he would add this: "For ye have heard of my conversation in time past in the Jews' religion, how that beyond measure I persecuted the church of God, and wasted it." (Galatians 1:13) What a transformation took place on that road to Damascus! For it was on that road that the persecutor Saul came face to face with the one he was really after, Jesus of Nazareth, and after that encounter the enemy of Jesus was changed into the evangelist for Christ.

Again in Saul's recorded testimony he wrote this: "But they had heard only, that he which persecuted us in times past now preacheth the faith which once he destroyed. And they glorified God in me." (Galatians 1:23-24) I have also thought in this switching of sides this would have been like the Germany General Erwin Rommel switching side on D-Day: the great Normandy landing of France! And yes at first there were skeptics about Saul's conversion; even the man that God sent to restore Saul's sight (Acts 9:8) was skeptical: "Then Ananias answered, Lord, I have heard by many of this man, how much evil he hath done to thy saints at Jerusalem: and here he hath authority from the chief priests to bind all that call on thy name." (Acts 9:13-14) But eventually by his change of life, living, and lifestyle and his preaching Christ (Acts 9:20) Saul convinced all men, friend and foe, that he had a genuine conversion. Saul would demonstrate something he would describe as: "Therefore if any man *be* in Christ, *he is* a new creature: old things are passed away; behold, all things are become new." (II Corinthians 5:17) This dramatic change took place because Jesus Christ Himself was still winning souls 'won by one'!

There seems to be a popular misconception that Jesus had left the evangelization of the world to the Church alone, and that He had a hands off approach after He ascended back to His Father. I believe the salvation of Saul puts that myth to bed. Weeks, months and could be said years and decades and millennium later is Jesus still leading people to Himself? We might not have many stories, and maybe someone else planted a seed or two, but I have during my life heard many a testimony of someone coming to Christ without anybody else being around. Jesus is still involved in evangelism, and like with Saul's story there are some people Jesus takes care of Himself. Saul would become a key figure in Jesus' plan for the expansion of the Church throughout the world. Remember what

Ananias was told to tell Saul: "But the Lord said unto him, Go thy way: for he is a chosen vessel unto me, to bear my name before the Gentiles, and kings, and the children of Israel: for I will shew him how great things he must suffer for my name's sake." (Acts 9:15-16) There was a great need for a tremendous turnaround in Saul's life if he would become what God wanted him to be, so Jesus took on this mission Himself. I have often wondered if Saul would have listened to anyone else but the Lord Jesus Christ Himself?

It is because of the unique way Saul came to know the Lord that I believe that Jesus is still in the direct conversion business: people that you or I could never reach; people in places where the Gospel has never been proclaimed, for even Saul had to be blinded. So Jesus often uses tragedy to open people's eyes to Himself; whereas at other times it is during times of depression and despair. Yes, I have read and heard personally various accounts from individuals that came to a saving knowledge of Jesus through Jesus' use of an event in their lives. Maybe not as dramatic as the sight Saul had on that site along the road to Damascus, but just as affective because salvation was the result. One of my favorite is the testimony of the great Irish preacher Willy Mullin who was converted one day not on a road but out in a field; alone, only him and God. After a very hard life of crime, he heard the voice of Jesus in that field outside of Belfast and falling on his knees he asked too 'what will you have me do'? Willy would go on to build one of the biggest Baptist churches in Ireland. Isn't it wonderful to know that Jesus is still winning souls!

Are you a vocal or perhaps a silent enemy of Jesus? Are you one of those hard nuts who have determined that the Christ isn't for you? Do you get a pleasure, or a joy out of persecuting the Christian you work with? Do you mock and make fun of any believer you come in contact with, either in your heart or verbally? I say watch out! For you might one day come into the category that I have been writing about in this chapter: a special handling of your life by Jesus Christ alone! Yes, you too can change sides even though you have been on the other side for a long time. Church history is filled with stories of the enemies of the Church, Christians, and the Christ who have changed sides. Those that were once agnostics, once atheists, once persecutors, once diehard unbelievers who would become faithful, dedicated followers of Jesus Christ and for many of them it was a personal intervention of Jesus Himself that made the difference. Your family and friends like them might not believe it at first, but like the demonic of the Gadarenes: "Return to thine own house, and shew how great things God hath done unto thee." (Luke 8:39) We often forget this description of Jesus by John: "And from Jesus Christ, **who is the faithful witness**, *and* the first begotten of the dead, and the prince of the kings of the earth." (Revelation 1:5) So the next time you take a walk down a road or a street it might not be a Christian that meets you along the way; it might just be Jesus Christ Himself! If Jesus wants you on His side, He might just approach you Himself with the invitation!

# 31

## WON: JETHRO THE MIDIANITE
## BY: Exodus 18:11

Now I know that the LORD *is* greater than all gods: for in the thing wherein they dealt proudly *he was* above them.

## ONE: MOSES

T. L. CUYLER WROTE this many years ago: "Years ago, before the city of London had modern paved streets, the story is told of an incident in Ruskin's life (John Ruskin-1819–1900, an English writer). He was known during his lifetime for never having missed an opportunity to relate the goodness of his God. While walking down one of the streets of London with a friend, the friend turned and disgustingly commended to Ruskin: 'What dirty, dreadful, loathsome compound, the mud of London streets.' 'Hold, my friend,' said Ruskin, 'Not so dreadful after all. What are the elements of this revolting substance? First, there is sand, but when its particles are crystalized according to the law of its nature, what is nicer than clean white sand? And when that which enters into it is arranged according to a still higher law, we have the matchless opal. What else have we in this mire? Clay. And to their higher laws, make the brilliant sapphire. What other ingredients enter into the London muck? Soot. And soot in its crystallized perfection forms the diamond. There is but one other: water; and water when distilled according to the higher law if its nature forms the dewdrops resting in exquisite perfection in the heart of the rose. So in the muddy, lost soul of man is hidden the image of his Creator, and God will do His best to find His opals, His sapphires,

His diamonds and His dewdrops. The heavenly treasury contains graces which can only be gathered one by one!'" What John Ruskin observed that day on the streets of London is a wonderful illustration of what we have been doing in this Biblical project of discovering God's opals and sapphires and diamond and dewdrops that have been collected for us to see in God's Holy Writ. In this chapter I would have us focus on Jethro, a gemstone of the faith that was first discovered in the mud of idolatry, the muck of paganism, and the mire of falsehood but won by one!

In Exodus 2:18 Jethro is called Reuel (God is Friend). In Numbers 10:29 and Judges 4:11 Jethro is called Hobab (beloved). Why these other names are mentioned in the Scriptural text we are not told; nicknames? But Jethro is the name given more often than not to Moses' father-in-law and Zipporah's father. Jethro was the priest and chief of a tribe of nomads called the Midianites. The Midianites were the descendants of a son born to Abraham and his third wife Keturah (remember Sarah and Hagar) named Midian (Genesis 25:1–2). The Midianites were a wandering clan of people who travelled the area of northern and southern Sinai. Like their forefathers they were shepherds moving from one grazing region to another. Remember, Moses became connected with the distant cousins after fleeing Egypt after his killing of the Egyptian task master (Exodus 2:15–17). After helping Jethro's oldest daughter in a dispute over water, Moses had been invited home by Zipporah to meet her father (Exodus 2:21–22). Having no sons, Jethro seems to adopt Moses and places him in charge of a flock of his sheep and for the next 40 years Moses settles into the lifestyle of the nomad traveling with Jethro and his family eventually marrying Zipporah and having a children. But what was the effect of Moses on Jethro in relationship to Jehovah God, especially after the burning bush incident? (Exodus 4:18) How did Moses influence the belief of this pagan priest/shepherd?

I have come to believe that after this encounter with God everything changed for Moses and I believe Jethro as well. Seemingly with Jethro's encouragement and blessing Moses returns to Egypt to deliver his people from their Egyptian task masters. Often we see conflict between a father-in-law and a son-in-law, but this doesn't seem to be the case as we read the events where Jethro and Moses interact. Being the head of the clan Jethro could have resisted Moses return to Egypt; Jethro was losing an important person in the tribe, a big gap seeing Moses was the only male in the immediate family. Jethro could have advised against the dangerous return, but he didn't; had something changed in Jethro's attitude about the Israelites and their God? In my research I have come to believe during that forty years in which Moses lived under the tent of Jethro that Moses had shared about the God of the Israelites and Jethro had been converted to a belief in the True and Living God. I was very blessed with a grand father-in-law in the person of Stacy Meister. Stacy had only been saved a short time when he started to attend my home church in Perham, Maine and I believe if he hadn't come to a belief in my Jesus I would never have meet his daughter. Did the same thing happen between Jethro and Moses?

Jethro is only mentioned once more in the Bible. Later after the dramatic events of the plagues and the deliverance from Egypt, and as the Israelites were working their way to Canaan by way of Mount Sinai (Exodus 3:12) the Midianites and Israelites meet. For a period of time it appears that the two clans travelled together, or they encamped together at the foot of Mount Sinai. It seems that the number one reason for the linking up of the clans was Jethro's return of his daughter (Zipporah) and his grandson (Gershom) to Moses. (Exodus 2:21–22) Seemingly, the pair had stayed with Jethro even though the text suggests that they started to Egypt with Moses (Exodus 4:20, 24–26). It was while Jethro was still in the Israelite camp that he noted that Moses was exhausting himself with the administration of the new nation. In some of the best advice on administration Jethro's advice was taken to the Lord and verified as being inspired because it was eventually written down by Moses in his history of the Jews (Exodus 18:13–26). One of the best examples of godly advice given in the Bible is the exchange between these two men over the responsibility of leadership. Over the years as a pastor I have also been placed in a position of advising people in a leadership role and I will be honest that I haven't found in the many books written about leadership anything better than Jethro's counsel! I am convinced that any good reading of Exodus 18 will also confirm my argument in this chapter that along with some great leadership precepts we have Jethro's confession that he had turned from worshipping the 'gods' of Midian to worshipping Jehovah. I think the verse that heads this chapter is the best prove there is. My conclusion is that Moses had been sent by God to Midian to win one, for often when the priest converts the people do.

Jethro seems to travel with Israel for a while acting as a desert guide (Numbers 10:29–32), even though the presence of God was still with the Israelites? (Exodus 13:21–22), but eventually Moses tells us that Jethro returns to the region of his nomadic life (Exodus 18:27), however, it does appear that some of the Midianites of Jethro's tribe decided to travel along with Israel to Canaan because they show up as the Kenites: "And the children of the Kenite, **Moses' father in law**, went up out of the city of palm trees with the children of Judah into the wilderness of Judah, which *lieth* in the south of Arad; and they went and dwelt among the people." (Judges 1:16) Probably the most famous was Jael the wife of Heber who killed the famous charioteer Sisera (Judges 4:11). I believe the faith of Jethro was passed on to his descendants: the precept of won by one goes on.

# 32

## WON: THE PALSY MAN
## BY: Mark 2:5

When Jesus saw their faith, he said unto the sick of the palsy, Son, thy sins be forgiven thee.

## ONE: THE PALSY MAN'S FRIENDS

THE BIBLE IS FILLED with stories about the unnamed, but not the unknown. Often we overlook these stories because the main characters are not named, but their stories are so unforgettable that we remember them forever. I have known the story of these five unnamed friends since childhood. Long before I could actually read their story myself, I could tell you their story. Unnamed often speaks of obscurity, unnoticed, the shadow people. So many fret and fuss over their limited talents, few possession, and feeble opportunities. Many go along in their daily routines, monotonous lives unacknowledged, unrecognized comforted only in the divine truth: ". . .for man looketh on the outward appearance, but the LORD looketh on the heart." (I Samuel 16:7) Is there any among us who could name one of Gideon's three hundred (Judges 7:6)? Personally, I can't believe that Gideon's servant Phurah (Judges 7:11) wasn't numbered among them? What of Elijah's seven thousand (I Kings 19:18)? Personally, I can't believe that Obadiah (I Samuel 18:3) wasn't numbered among them? And what about the heroes in this chapter, the friends of the palsy man that brought him to Jesus; any names? But in these stories and many others scattered throughout the Bible a valuable lesson is being highlighted and underlined: it is far better to be faithful then famous! It is in our story we learn another valuable virtue that isn't mentioned much, but I believe is very important: group faith; something I believe Paul talks about in his famous chapter on faith: "By faith **they** passed through the Red sea as by dry *land*: which the Egyptians assaying to do were drowned. By faith the walls of Jericho fell down, after they were compassed about seven days." (Hebrews 11:29-30) The 'they' is a group, and the five friends had this faith because the text is clear above: 'Jesus saw **their** faith'! I believe that our precept of 'won by one' is still intact in this story because the one is a group of 4, a group faith that brought their friend to Jesus, and again the story doesn't start with a healing, but a conversion!

Not only is this a story of the unnamed, but it is a story of the unknowns: an unknown house, an unknown host, and four unknown helpers. Despite these unknowns there are enough knows to reveal to us the truths at the heart of this story. I make these observation based on my understanding of the story (Romans 14:5). First, there had to be great **charity**, if not love between these five friends. The concern of the four over the fifth drove them to seek out this healer they had heard about, and their compassion for their mural friend's condition. Second, there had to be a **unity** among them for without team work and cooperation and coordination the task would never have been accomplished. Third, there had to be a kind of **tenacity,** a perseverance, persistence in the group, for there were enough obstacles to have discouraged them from continuing like they did. Fourth, there must have been **ingenuity** for who figured out the alternative route to Jesus? And finally there must have been an **urgency** in the group. It seems throughout the telling of this tale the one overriding aspect seemed to motivate this quartet that setbacks, stumbling blocks, and obstacles couldn't stop; and that one motivation: getting their friend to the feet of Jesus. Without them the palsy man would never have reached Jesus!

Yet as Mark tells the story the only thing Jesus recognized in all of this was not their charity, their unity, their tenacity, their ingenuity, or their urgency; it was their faith! Again it wasn't his faith, but their faith. It was the faith of the five not the one. I think what we have here is the precept written about by Jesus' brother James: "And the prayer of faith shall save the sick, and the Lord shall raise him up; and if he have committed sins, they shall be forgiven him." (James 5:15) Remember, the first words out of the mouth of Jesus weren't: "I say unto thee, Arise, and take up thy bed, and go thy way into thine house." (Mark 2:11) The first words from Jesus' lips were: ". . .Son, thy sins be forgiven thee." (Mark 2:5) The most important thing you could do for your sick friend is to take his case to the throne of God and the same is true about your unsaved friend. So many get their priorities in these cases reversed. What good is an earthly healing without a spiritual healing? So many today are going to hell in perfect bodily health!

For me, there was much to learn about these five friends and their faith:

1. Theirs was an UNASSUMING FAITH. Someone other than themselves was at the forefront of their attention. The center of their attraction was the need of their mutual friend, the one that needed their help. Despite 'their faith', Jesus focused on 'son', as if the others were already believers? There is still the unanswered question of how much more could be accomplished in the Body of Christ if each member didn't care who got the credit, the glory? There is no telling how many more people could receive salvation if we would focus on the sinner not the statistics. I still remember the competition in souls being saved in the 1970s!

2. Theirs was an UORTHODOX FAITH. Whatever it takes to get your friend to Jesus. Oh, we have restricted ourselves to this plan or that, this method or that; the Church needs to think outside of the traditional box. Read your Church history and you will find that Paul was unorthodox and so was Hudson Taylor and William Carey. The "Won by One" champions of the Church have been creative to say the least to getting the Gospel to those who need Jesus Christ as Saviour.

3. Theirs was an UNRECOGNIZED FAITH. Think with me. To the majority of the people that were in the room with Jesus, and those outside looking in all they could see was the palsy man lying on his bed. Jesus only spoke to the palsy man, not the friends. Granted, they must have looked around when the man suddenly appeared before Jesus, but the focus soon switched because of the controversy (read Mark 2:6–10). The principle we need to highlight and underline here is the fact, who cares who gets the credit, for Jesus will see your faithfulness and helpfulness and that should be enough. Don't forget God does see that unwitnessed act of kindness to that widow next door; that unseen gift to the needy neighbor; and that unacknowledged faithfulness to that orphan in another country. They all have been recorded in the books of heaven and one day everybody will know about it: "Likewise also the good works *of some*

are manifest beforehand; and they that are otherwise cannot be hid." (I Timothy 5:25)

Any time you are called on to help the helpless God is always there. It might be in the middle of the night when no one sees or recognizes your deed, but Jesus sees, and one day hopefully not too far into the distant future you will hear: "...well done thou good and faithful servant..." (Matthew 25:23) Who knows after the meeting was over that Jesus didn't find the four lads and told them just that? Today Jesus is still looking for the faithful not the famous (I Corinthians 1:26–29), so let us get about His business!

## 33

## WON: URIAH THE HITTITE
## BY: II Samuel 11:11

And Uriah said unto David, The ark, and Israel, and Judah, abide in tents; and my lord Joab, and the servants of my lord, are encamped in the open fields; shall I then go into mine house, to eat and to drink, and to lie with my wife? *as* thou livest, and *as* thy soul liveth, I will not do this thing.

## ONE: DAVID

THE HITTITES WERE THE descendants of Heth, the second son of Canaan. (Genesis 10:15) They were a peaceful and commercial people when they are first mentioned in the Scriptures as they sold to Father Abraham a burial place for his beloved wife Sarah (Genesis 23:7–10). It seems as with the Amorites in battle (Genesis 14:13), Abraham took the Hittites as commercial allies in business, and at the first there seemed to be no bad blood between the races! However, by the time Joshua and the armies of Israel arrived in Canaan to claim their Promised land by conquest, the Hittites were well established in the mountain country that would become the possession of the Tribe of Judah. They were numbered with the "....seven nations greater and mightier than. . .." countries on God's hit list (Deuteronomy 7:1). Often times in the listing of these seven nations, the Hittites are named first (Deuteronomy 20:17). Why they rose to the top of God's list we know not? So when the Israelites failed to utterly destroy the Hittites a door was opened to reveal the most honorable Hittite of them all and certainly the most mentioned Hittite in Biblical history: the unsuspicious, self-denying, loyal, and honorable patriot in

David's army: Uriah the Hittite, the husband of Bathsheba, and "Jehovah is Light"!

Uriah, though a descendant of a cursed race, was himself a devote follower of David and I believe David's God. He came up through the ranks until he attained a position numbered among David's elite trooper known as the 'thirty' (I Chronicles 11:41 and II Samuel 23:39). It is interesting to note, as we have before, in the listing of these warriors that many of David's special soldiers were actually foreigners: Ittai, a Philistine, Ithmah the Moabite, and Zelek the Ammonite, but the most famous of the lot was Uriah the Hittite. The conclusion I have reached as I have surveyed these names is that David was looking for the best of the best no matter where they were from or what race they were from. Character and courage were the qualities David looked for, more than culture!

The Scripture is not clear when Uriah meet and married the beautiful Bathsheba, or when Uriah joined David's Band and became one of his top officers, yet both these situation play a part in the tragic tale that will unfold in Uriah's life. This story centers on this marriage and Uriah's loyalty and devotion despite the intrigue and suspicion that results in one of the most dramatic accounts of Holy Writ. For me, it is again in the meaning of Uriah that I have gotten insight for this devotional. Uriah means "Jehovah is Light". Uriah's devote and tender devotion for Bathsheba is seen in Nathan's description of Bathsheba in his parable: "But the poor man (Uriah) had nothing except one little ewe (Bathsheba) lamb he had bought. He raised it, and it grew up with him and his children. It shared his food, drank from his cup, and even slept in his arms. It was like a daughter to him." (II Samuel 12:3 NIV) Despite being the apple of his eye and the love of his life, Bathsheba was second on Uriah's love list, for he loved his king even more! To me we have before us how we are to love our Lord and King, Jesus Christ. Do you love Him more than anyone, or anything else? (John 21:15) Love and loyalty cannot be separated! Many forces try, but a genuine love and a faithful loyalty will win every time; will conquer every time even if in the end death comes to the champion of loyalty!

The story book romance takes a bitter and tragic twist when while Uriah is off fighting the king's battle (II Samuel 11:1). As Uriah fights a dangerous and difficult siege of Rabbah, his king and his wife have an adulterous affair resulting in Bathsheba becoming pregnant with the King's child! To cover up the wickedness David hatches a plot to grant Uriah a special furlough from the battlefront in a vain attempt to make

Uriah, not David, appear to be the father of Bathsheba's unborn baby. Though unaware of the scheme, Uriah demonstrates a quality trait rarely seen in the Bible, let alone in the world. For at a moment's notice, Uriah's soldierly devotion and chivalrous character comes shining through: "Uriah says to David, the ark, and Israel and Judah are staying in tents, and my master Joab (his commanding officer) and my lord's men are camped in the open fields. How could I go to my house to eat, and drink, and lie with my wife. As surely as you live I will not do such a thing." (II Samuel 11:17 NIV) Truly, a man in whom David was not worthy, but a man that is worthy of the name "Jehovah is Light". So to cover and hid his shame and sin, David uses Uriah's loyalty and love to destroy him!

Unable to frame Uriah and unable to keep concealed his transgression, David plots a second time, a plan B if you will. David will turn the courage and bravery of Uriah into an instrument of murder: "In the morning David wrote a letter to Joab and sent it with Uriah. In it he wrote, Put Uriah in the front line where the fighting is fiercest. Then withdraw from him so he will be struck down and die." (II Samuel 11:15–15 NIV) In the daily war correspondence between Joab and David, Joab simply wrote at the end of the dispatch: "And Uriah the Hittite died also." (II Samuel 11:17 KJV) It is worth noting that what David ordered and what Joab did are not quite the same (Compare II Samuel 11:15 and 16). David ordered a retreat, an abandonment of Uriah; while Joab simply put Uriah in the hottest part of the battle, up against the best soldiers of Rabbah. Did Joab follow the order of David to the letter of the law, or did he give Uriah a fighting chance against the best warriors of their enemy? I think this is another one of those situations where each must make up his own mind on this matter (Romans 14:5).

Loyal unto death and totally unaware, I believe, of the cloak and dagger plot whirling around him. Uriah is a good example of a "sealed orders" kind of faith (Hebrews 11:8). As Abraham left Haran 'not knowing where he was going', Uriah left Jerusalem 'not knowing he had been ordered to die'. I hear a lot people saying that wasn't fair, and it wasn't, but Uriah was right; he did the right thing. It would have been dishonorable to have read the dispatch, and for the life of Uriah he never would have because in the mighty plan of God; Uriah was expendable. I hear a lot saying I would never let anyone misuse and abuse me like that, yet the Lord taught: "And if someone wants to sue you and take your tunic, let him have your cloak as well. If someone forces you to go one mile, go with him two miles." (Matthew 5:40–41) Our loyalty and honor reaches to God not government, to our King not our kinsmen. It is a far better thing to be faithful unto death, than to be disloyal in life. I believe when Nathan finally exposed David's sin and when he said: "You are the man!" (II Samuel 12:7 NIV), I believe that David would have traded places with Uriah; for the light of Jehovah shone brightly in the mighty man Uriah.

So the man who led Uriah to God, was the man in the end that signed his death warrant!!!

# 34

## WON: NEBUCHADNEZZAR THE BABYLONIAN
## BY: Daniel 4:37

Now I Nebuchadnezzar praise and extol and honour the King of heaven, all whose works *are* truth, and his ways judgment: and those that walk in pride he is able to abase.

## ONE: DANIEL

F. B. MEYER, IN his book "Great Verses Through the Bible", writes this about Nebuchadnezzar's confession written above: "This is the confession of a heathen king; but how true it is, and how well for us, if we dare to affirm, amid all the appearances to the contrary, and all the shrinking in the natural man, that all God's works are truth and His ways righteous, not only in the wide circumference of the heavens, but in the tiny circle of our little life. The main lesson, let us note it, which this chapter is designed to teach, and which Nebuchadnezzar epitomizes in these words, is abhorrence with which God regards pride. We are all tempted to walk on the terrace of our palace, and say, 'Is not this great Babylon which I have built by the might of my power and for the glory of my majesty?' (Daniel 4:30) But to speak thus is to incur the displeasure of the Most High, who giveth the kingdom to whosoever He will (Daniel 2:21). If thou hast achieved a position of wealth and independence and success (Deuteronomy 8:17–18), do not be proud of it, as though it were all of thy own creating. God gave thee power to get wealth; raised thee to that responsible position (Psalm 75:6–7) as His agent and trustee; and made thy name as one of the great over the earth. Give Him the glory, and be sure to consider thyself only as His steward, entrusted with His property, and continued in thy position for as long a time as thou art faithful in thine administration. May not that illness, that suspension from active work, that serious deprivation, have been sent to thee, as this madness was permitted to come to the king of Babylon, that thou shouldest know and acknowledge that the heaven do rule? Remember that the watchers and the holy ones still walk the world with viewless footprints, and give in their account your deeds to Him!"

Beside the hand of God put on Nebuchadnezzar for his pride, I believe he had a young man in his kingdom whose testimony also brought him to an understanding and an acceptance of the True and Living God. The Bible is clear: "For ye see your calling, brethren, how that not many wise men after the flesh, not many mighty, not many noble, *are called*: but God hath chosen the foolish things of the world to confound the wise; and God hath chosen the weak things of the world to confound the things which are mighty; and base things of the world, and things which are despised, hath God chosen, *yea*, and things which are not, to bring to nought things that are: that no flesh should glory in his presence." (I Corinthians 1:26–29) These verses might say 'not many', but as someone once observed, it doesn't say 'not any'! And I believe that one of the exceptions to God rule was the mighty Babylonian King Nebuchadnezzar , and his coming to God is another one of our 'won by one' stories of the Bible and the 'one' was the amazing Daniel!

If there was a man who came the closest to these questions by Jesus it was King Nebuchadnezzar: "For what is a man profited, if he shall gain the whole world, and lose his own soul? or what shall a man give in exchange for his soul?" (Matthew 16:26) Even God Himself recognized Nebuchadnezzar as the greatest ruler of all the ancient kingdom of the world. There were emperors who controlled more land than Nebuchadnezzar ever controlled. There were empires that lasted longer than Nebuchadnezzar's kingdom. There were kings greater in battle than Nebuchadnezzar was in war, but when it came to supreme control and personal power before or after nobody every match Nebuchadnezzar according to God: "And wheresoever the children of men dwell, the beasts of the field and the fowls of the heaven hath he given into thine hand, and hath made thee ruler over them all. Thou *art* this head of gold." (Daniel 2:38) Even the mighty Roman Empire, despite its longevity, expansion, and dominance was only 'iron' compared to 'gold' (Daniel 3:39). All before and after were second rate at best compared to Nebuchadnezzar, and it appears that God was determined to bring this arrogant king into his fold, and He would do anything to achieve that including sending a young, godly, faithful Hebrew from his homeland, into captivity, made a eunuch, to teach a prideful king about Jehovah!

However, Nebuchadnezzar, like most kings or politicians before and after, when faced with prosperity and prestige and power were tempted becoming proud and pompous. When Nebuchadnezzar heard from God Himself that he was that head of gold he made an image I believe of himself, but in great arrogance made the complete image of gold boldly proclaiming that his empire would never fall! Then Nebuchadnezzar demanded that everybody worship the image, or worship him as a god! (Daniel 3:1) Nebuchadnezzar wasn't the first or the last king to make himself god. Read what happened to King Herod when he decided to accept the attribute of divinity by his subjects (Acts 12:20-23)! Through Daniel God warned Nebuchadnezzar of his growing pride (Daniel 4:1-27), just like God warned Cain about his growing anger against his brother (Genesis 4:6-7), but just like Cain Nebuchadnezzar failed to heed the warning. Sometimes a human instrument is not enough; sometimes a human example is not enough and God has to step in personally as He did according to Daniel 4:28-33!!!!!!

God had given Nebuchadnezzar years of grace (Daniel 4:29), but in the end pride had taken over so before the words of pride get out of his mouth God's voice was heard by the arrogant king. It took seven long and difficult years before we have this testimony by Nebuchadnezzar himself: "And at the end of the days I Nebuchadnezzar lifted up mine eyes unto heaven, and mine understanding returned unto me, and I blessed the most High, and I praised and honoured him that liveth for ever, whose dominion *is* an everlasting dominion, and his kingdom *is* from generation to generation." (Daniel 4:34) With the wicked and powerful spirit of pride broken, Nebuchadnezzar confessed and acknowledged that it was God and God alone who had given him all that he had. It was Nebuchadnezzar's greatest conquest, and Nebuchadnezzar become one of God's greatest converts, for he immediately made know the Lord God throughout his lands: "And all the inhabitants of the earth *are* reputed as nothing: and he doeth according to his will in the army of heaven, and *among* the inhabitants of the earth: and none can stay his hand, or say unto him, What doest thou? At the same time my reason returned unto me; and for the glory of my kingdom, mine honour and brightness returned unto me; and my counsellors and my lords sought unto me; and I was established in my kingdom, and excellent majesty was added unto me." (Daniel 4:35–26) Won by One again!

Maybe you are caught in the grip of pride, and maybe God will have to take away what He has given you so that you might know Him? I believe God has put His witness somewhere around us who has been sharing with you the knowledge of God with you. Listen to them before God has to intervene. Read carefully I Corinthians 11:31–32! And "...he saith, God resisteth the proud, but giveth grace unto the humble!" (James 4:6)

# 35

## WON: SIMON THE CYRENIAN
## BY: Matthew 27:32

And as they came out, they found a man of Cyrene, Simon by name: him they compelled to bear his cross.

## ONE: JESUS

THE BIBLE GIVES US many men by the name of Simon. There was Simon Peter the famous (John 1:41) and Simon the sorcerer the infamous (Acts 8:9). There was the other disciple of Jesus named Simon (Matthew 10:4) and the other brother of Jesus named Simon (Mark 6:3). There was a leper named Simon (Matthew 26:6), and a Pharisee named Simon (Luke 7:36). Judas Iscariot's father's name was Simon (John 6:71), and there was a tanner in the Book of Acts called Simon (Acts 9:43). And then there was Simon of Cyrene; a man known in the Bible for only one thing. A man seemingly caught at the wrong time and in the wrong place, or was he? Simon's one memorable, Scriptural act certainly qualifies him for the theme of this book. Unexpected and probably unprepared, Simon was instantaneously thrust into the most dramatic trek in history: Jesus walk to Golgotha's brow, but in the end he got save!

Some call it fate, but I call it fantastic. It was not mere chance or circumstance that Simon was where he was on that fateful morning; just like it was not by chance or circumstance that Esther was queen of Persia at the time of Haman's devilish plot. Mordecai's great question applied to Esther but I also believe to Simon: *"...and who knoweth whether thou art come to the kingdom for such a time as this?"* (Esther 4:14) I also believe it was not by chance or circumstance that Joseph was prime minister of Egypt at the time of the great Egyptian Famine. What did Joseph tell his brothers? "Now therefore be not grieved, nor angry with yourselves, that ye sold me hither: for God did send me before you to preserve life." (Genesis 45:5) God does not deal in chance or circumstance! I have always loved the story of King Ahab and his death on the battlefield of Ramoth-Gilead. Remember the little known prophet Micaiah predicted that Ahab would die in the up and coming battle, but Ahab through he would outsmart God by going into the battle disguised, yet we read: "And a *certain* man drew a bow at a venture, and smote the king of Israel between the joints of the harness: wherefore he said unto the driver of his chariot, Turn thine hand, and carry me out of the host; for I am wounded." (I Kings 22:34) We forget that God is in control of every arrow that flies in battle and every pilgrim who comes to Jerusalem to celebrate the Passover festival!

Granted, I would believe that Simon had come for the celebration and not to help a condemned man carry his cross to a crucifixion. I believe Simon probably resisted at first because of the words in our key verse above: "they compelled him"! Simon was forced by the Roman soldiers, probably by sword point, to help Jesus; an unknown man to Simon at the time. No doubt Simon was picked at random by the Romans after the numerous falls by Jesus under the heavy load. The soldiers were in a hurry to get the gruesome task over and Jesus was slowing up the process. The Romans selected Simon, but I believe God chose him: "For the gifts and calling of God *are* without repentance." (Romans 11:29) And in the end I believe the cross-sharing assignment was the greatest event in Simon's life. What a marvellous fate when Jesus is involved, and what was true of Simon of Cyrene I believe is true of every one of us when God chooses us to walk with His Son, the Lord Jesus Christ.

John Mark, in his glorious Gospel, adds something to Simon's account that the other Gospel writers didn't mention: "And they compel one Simon a Cyrenian, who passed by, coming out of the country, **the father of Alexander and Rufus**, to bear his cross." (Mark 15:21) Mark writes of Simon's boys as if his reader would recognize the children's names rather than the father's name? Where, at the time of Mark's Gospel, Alexander and Rufus well-known members of the early Church: "Salute Rufus chosen in the Lord and his mother and mine?" (Romans 16:13) I think that most feel as I do that if Jesus witness to the thief on the cross (Luke 23:39–43) then He also witnessed to Simon on the Via-Delarosa? In my own personal opinion (II Peter 1:20), I believe that like the thief on the cross Simon got saved that day and took the Gospel to his boys. I don't know if like Ray Bolt's song "The Lamb" says that Alexander and Rufus were with their father that day in Jerusalem, but I do believe that eventually they too came to a saving knowledge of Jesus Christ by the experience of their father's sharing Jesus' cross. We know nothing else about Simon of Cyrene, for as quickly as he comes on the pages of Holy Writ he disappears, but his single act of cross-sharing does teach us much about bearing and sharing His cross in our service of our Lord and Saviour Jesus Christ!

Long before Simon helped Jesus with His cross, Jesus was teaching His disciples: "Then said Jesus unto his disciples, If any *man* will come after me, let him deny himself, and take up his cross, and follow me." (Matthew 16:24) Saints are called like Simon to be cross-bearers. Christ didn't bear the cross so that His followers could escape it, but to teach us how to endure it. I see a four-fold lesson in the example of Simon of Cyrene. One, as with Simon, **it is not our cross, but Christ's cross that we bear**! "And whosoever doth not bear *His cross*, and come after me, cannot be my disciple." (Luke 14:27) Have you given your soul to Jesus, but you have yet to take up His cross, His cause in your life? (Romans 12:1) Two, as with Simon, **we carry His cross behind Him not before Him**! "And as they led him away, they laid hold upon one Simon, a Cyrenian, coming out of the country, and on him they laid the cross, *that he might bear it after Jesus*." (Luke 23:26) Always remember that Jesus will never direct you to a path that He Himself hasn't already walked (I John 2:6). Third, as with Simon, **do not forget that you bear the cross in partnership**! "I am crucified with Christ: nevertheless I live; yet not I, but Christ liveth in me: and *the life which I now live in the flesh I live by the faith of the Son of God*, who loved me, and gave himself for me." (Galatians 2:20) And remember, this burden is light and the yoke is easy because we share the load together (Matthew 11:28–30). Four, as with Simon, **thought he only carried the cross for a short time; it has given him an eternal weight of glory**! "For our light affliction, which is but for a moment, *worketh for us a far more exceeding and eternal weight of glory*." (II Corinthians 4:17) And as a dear saint once said: **"We must be cross bearers before we can be crown wearers!"** (James 1:12) It was the Apostle Paul who believed: "For I reckon that the sufferings of this present time *are* not worthy *to be compared* with the glory which shall be revealed in us." (Romans 8:18) Despite Simon's one at a moment's notice, his example has inspired saints down through the ages to also faithfully take up Jesus' cross and bear it and share it with others, but before you can bear His cross you must first believe on Him and what He did for you on Calvary; I believe like Simon did on that difficult road to the cross, but that terrible walk brought him to Christ (I John 2:6).

# 36

**WON:** THE PHILIPPI DAMSEL
**BY:** Acts 16:18

And this did she many days. But Paul, being grieved, turned and said to the spirit, I command thee in the name of Jesus Christ to come out of her. And he came out the same hour.

**ONE:** PAUL

THERE SEEMS TO BE a popular misconception floating around these days that the Devil and his demons have free well in matters pertaining to their evil work! I have heard recently of a suggestion that the wicked forces prevalent in this age have no concept of God and they pretty much do as they please. Once again these beliefs are propagated by an ignorance of the Bible. The world has forgotten James 2:19: "Thou believest that there is one God; thou doest well: the devils also believe, and tremble." I have come to believe that Satan and his spirits live in a constant fear of the Almighty and what He could do to them at any moment. I know the Devil and his demons act rough, and seem to be in control, but this is far, far from the truth, or reality. Remember what the reactions of the demons were when Jesus confronted the spirits of the Gergesenes demonic? "And, behold, they cried out, saying, what have we to do with thee, Jesus, thou Son of God? Art thou come hither to torment us before the time?" (Matthew 8:29) I believe what is true of the Christ should be true of the Christian. We fear them; they ought to be fearing us, and to illustrate this truth I would like to share this 'won by one' story out of the life of the Apostle Paul and the experience he and Silas had in Philippi.

Paul and Silas were making spiritual inroads in Europe for the first time when they came face to face with a demon possessed girl: "And it came to pass, as we went to prayer, a certain damsel possessed with a spirit of divination met us, which brought her masters much gain by soothsaying." (Acts 16:16) Let me make this very clear from the outset and that being that wegeboards, terra cards, soothsaying, crystal balls, 'dungeons and dragons', and the like are all demonic instruments. Demonology is alive and well as it was that day in Philippi when Paul and Silas and Luke (note the 'us' in Acts 16:17-Luke was there, the author of this book) meet this girl. The power of the mediums, witches, fortune tellers and the like can be traced to Satan himself and his cronies. The occult and spiritism are on the rise today because the Devil and his demons know their time is short, so that is why it is important to set this question to rest, because if the demons knew the Christ, they know the followers of the Christ: "The same followed Paul and us, and cried, saying, These men are the servants of the most high God, which shew unto us the way of salvation." (Acts 16:17) The Devil knows where to find you and so does his followers. We are marked out in the crowd just like the trio that was evangelizing Philippi (read Acts 16:12–15). Remember the story of Job when God and Satan meet and Satan tried to pretend that he wasn't after Job; God quickly put Satan right (Job 1:8). Satan knew Job well because he had been hunting and hounding him for years, but couldn't get at him because of God's hedge (Job 1:10). Satan has always had his henchmen harassing the saints of God, and in Philippi the demon was in the girl. As the story goes eventually Paul had had enough, but note Paul didn't turn on the damsel but the demon: "And this did she many days. But Paul, being grieved, turned and said to the spirit, I command thee in the name of Jesus Christ to come out of her. And he came out the same hour." (Acts 16:18) Paul recognized that the problem was the demon of divination, not the poor damsel that had been taken over by the demon. I have come to believe that many of the out-of-control people of this world that do demonic things are also controlled by wicked spirits. The cure is a simple one: bringing in the Spirit of God will drive out the spirit of Satan!

Paul simply did what Jesus told his followers to do: "And these signs shall follow them that believe; *In my name shall they cast out devils*; they shall speak with new tongues." (Mark 16:17) And in the name of Jesus the spirit left, it has to leave, just like Satan must stop bothering you if you simply resist him: "Submit yourselves therefore to God. **Resist the devil, and he will flee from you.**" (James 4:7) There can be no argument, no debate, no complaints because the demons and the Devil have no rights or power to resist the name of Jesus. How the Church of God needs to relearn this lesson, for we seem to be paralyzed with fear against spiritual wickedness in high places (read Ephesians 6:10–18 again)! We live in a world that tolerates wickedness, co-exists with evil, putting up with wrongs when all we have to do is take a stand like Paul and put those demons to flight. I love the other encounter recorded by Luke in Acts 19:13–16: "Then certain of the vagabond Jews, exorcists, took upon them to call over them which had evil spirits the name of the Lord Jesus, saying, We adjure you by Jesus whom Paul preacheth. And there were seven sons of *one* Sceva, a Jew, *and* chief of the priests, which did so. And the evil spirit answered and said, Jesus I know, and Paul I know; but who are ye? And the man in whom the evil spirit was leaped on them, and overcame them, and prevailed against them, so that they fled out of that house naked and wounded." Warning you should think seriously about standing with Christ before you use his name (Matthew 7:21–23). There is only power in Jesus' name if Jesus knows you, not if you think you know him. What makes this truth so real is this instruction by John: "Ye are of God, little children, and have overcome them: **because greater is he that is in you, than he that is in the world.**" (I John 4:4) Paul knew this in Philippi, but I believe something else wonderfully happened when that demon was chased away from the girl, and I am not taking about the arrest, the imprisonment, and the more famous conversion!

I believe if Paul lead Lydia and her family to a saving knowledge of Christ (Acts 16:13–15) and Paul lead the Philippian jailer and his family to a saving knowledge of Jesus Christ (Acts 16:30–34) why can't we believe that Paul lead this damsel to the Lord? I have come to believe that this girl became a charter member in the First Church of Philippi because Paul knew that even a demon couldn't stop a conversion. Wouldn't this damsel have seen the change in her life and wouldn't she have sought the answer for her deliverance not only from the demon but those that were exploiting her (Acts 16:19)? I feel we have a marvelous example for those who want a cure from drink and drugs and other additive things, for they are like demon-possession. What Paul did for that damsel in Philippi we too can do for those who are possessed in our age? The name of Jesus was the answer then and it still is the answer now. I love what the early disciples said to Jesus after they returned from their first mission trips into their world: "And the seventy returned again with joy, saying, Lord, even **the devils are subject unto us through thy name.**" (Luke 10:17)

When will we stop walking around in fear of the demons of our world? Remember they fear the name of Jesus, they fear those that follow Jesus, but this seems to be the best kept secret in the Church of the Living God. Remember where Jesus send the demons who came out of the man of the Gergesenes (Matthew 8:28–31)? Pigs!

# 37

## WON: LYDIA THE THYATIRIAN
## BY: Acts 16:14

And a certain woman named Lydia, a seller of purple, of the city of Thyatira, which worshipped God, heard *us*: whose heart the Lord opened, that she attended unto the things which were spoken of Paul.

## ONE: PAUL

THE LORD THROUGH THE Hebrew prophet Jeremiah told us: "The heart is deceitful above all things, and desperately wicked", but then Jeremiah asked, "And who can know it?" (Jeremiah 17:9) Seemingly in answer to his own question Jeremiah also wrote this: "I the Lord search the heart, I try the reins, even to give every man according to his ways, and according to the fruit of his doing." (Jeremiah 17:10) I believe such was the case in Philippi as God scanned the hearts of its inhabitants and found a lady by the name of Lydia; a woman who at a moment's notice opened her heart up to the teachings of the Apostle Paul and got gloriously saved. Like the other individuals I have been highlighting and underlining in this devotional book, Lydia is only mentioned once in the Holy Bible, but her act of faith took her from her business profession and changed her vocation: "I therefore, the prisoner of the Lord, beseech you that ye walk worthy of the vocation wherewith ye are called." (Ephesians 4:1) Has that happened to you as of yet?

John Hall once wrote this after watching a flower open and close: "The buds had hung with closed pedals all day, but towards evening they opened and released a pleasing aroma. As I observed this 'miracle' of nature, it was more than I had anticipated. A silent awe come over men as bud after bud slowly curled back before my eyes. As if touched by an invisible hand, the vine was soon aglow with beautiful, fragrant blossoms. If the finger of God laid open these flowers can do this in a way beyond the power of man to explain, cannot the same divine touch do so much for the human heart?" I too have seen this affect in the medical field. As a pastor for over fifty years, I have had my share of parishioners with heart issues. Many of them in the four churches that I have pastored have had to have open-heart procedures done. Before they go into the operating room their lives are filled with weakness, shortness of breath, pain, and often despair. But after a gifted surgeon is finished with their operation their lives were characterized by energy, health and hope for a longer life. Is not that what took place on the shores of that river in Philippi the day the Master spiritual surgeon opened Lydia's heart by the scalpel in the hands of Paul and the moving of the Spirit of God? A poet has written: "An operation all divine, by God's own Spirit given, now only can implant in men, a new heart fit for heaven." Ezekiel knew of that new heart when he wrote: "Then will I sprinkle clean water upon you, and ye shall be clean: from all your filthiness, and from all your idols, will I cleanse you. A new heart also will I give you, and a new spirit will I put within you: and I will take away the stony heart out of your flesh, and I will give you an heart of flesh. And I will put my spirit within you, and cause you to walk in my statutes, and ye shall keep my judgments, and do *them*. And ye shall dwell in the land that I gave to your fathers; and ye shall be my people, and I will be your God." (Ezekiel 36:25-28)

In Charles Spurgeon's comments on the conversion of Lydia in his devotional book "Evening and Morning", he makes these interesting statements: "Observe the words: 'whose heart the Lord opened.' She did not open her own heart. Her prayers did not do it; Paul did not do it. The Lord Himself must open the heart, to receive the things which make for our peace. He alone can put the key into the hole of the door and open it, and get admittance for Himself. He is the heart's Master as He is the heart's Maker. The first outward evidence of the opened heart was obedience. As soon as Lydia had believed in Jesus, she was baptized. ("And when she was baptized, and her household, she besought *us*, saying, if ye have judged me to be faithful to the Lord, come into my house, and abide *there*. And she constrained us." Acts 16:15) It is a sweet sign of a humble and broken heart when the child of God is willing to obey a command which is not essential to her salvation, which is not forced upon her by a selfish fear of condemnation, but a simple act of obedience and of communion with her Master. Those who do nothing for Christ or His Church, give but sorry evidence of an 'open heart'. Lord, evermore give me an opened heart!" This ought to be our prayer as well, especially if we are not saved. Again, unless the Good Lord touches our heart there will be no redemption, no renewal, and no reformation. Many people try with diet or exercise or lifestyle change to fix a damaged heart, but as with a spiritual heart only a major surgery will do. But if you will like Lydia permit the knife of the Word of God ("For the word of God *is* quick, and powerful, and sharper than any twoedged sword, piercing even to the dividing asunder of soul and spirit, and of the joints and marrow, and *is* a discerner of the thoughts and intents of the heart." Hebrews 4:12) to open you up so that the transforming power of the Holy Spirit ("Therefore if any man *be* in Christ, *he is* a new creature: old things are passed away; behold, all things are become new." II Corinthians 5:17) can give you a new heart! Have you a new heart yet?

Notice however, the process unlike open heart surgery did not take weeks of preparation or hours of surgery. As F. B. Meyer so graphically put it years ago in his book "Great Verses through the Bible": "Lydia's heart opened as a flower beneath the touch of the sun, so gradually and imperceptibly that it was impossible to say the precise moment of her new life?" A distinguished missionary once said: "The Lord awakened me with a kiss!" It was as if Lydia's heart had awakened from a deep spiritual sleep (Ephesians 2:1). Too often we only look for the outward signs and manifestations of something happening, when in reality without our knowing a transformation, a transfiguration is taking place inside. Did Lydia go to the river that day to get save? Probably not, but the undeniable moving of God was playing its part that day bringing sinner and salvation together. Many don't go to church to get converted, yet they get converted. The morning I received the Lord Jesus Christ as my Saviour I got up like I had so many times before to a Sunday morning on the homestead. I did my chores before I put on my Sunday best and travelled the three miles to the little white church on the corner in downtown Perham. I went downstairs for children's church as my parents stayed upstairs for the morning service of the First Baptist Church. Little did I know that I was in for a heart change before that service was over? All it took was a moment when the Father called (John 6:37) and the Spirit convicted (John 16:8) and the Son converted (Matthew 18:3). Such was the case with Lydia and such was the case with me. What a wonderful change had taken place, and she is mentioned at the end of this story, after Paul and Silas' release from jail Luke writes: "And they went out of the prison, and entered into *the house of* Lydia: and when they had seen the brethren, they comforted them, and departed." (Acts 16:40) The words of an old Church hymn starts: "What a wonderful change in my life has wrought since Jesus came into my heart......" Could I ask you once again have you had a spiritual heart operation yet? God is ready to change you!

# 38

**WON:** SIMON THE CANAANITE
**BY:** Mark 3:18

And Andrew, and Philip, and Bartholomew, and Matthew, and Thomas, and James the *son* of Alphaeus, and Thaddaeus, and Simon the Canaanite.

**ONE:** JESUS

SIMON THE CANAANITE, THE disciple (Matthew 10:1–4) and later the apostle for Jesus Christ (Luke 6:13–16), is the only Canaanite mentioned in the New Testament. Canaanite is the patronymic of the descendants of Canaan (Genesis 10:6), but for most of the Old Testament this term is restricted to the inhabitants of Canaan, the old Promise Land of the Hebrews. So was Simon the disciple a Canaanite by race or by region? I will leave that debate with you (Romans 14:5), for the focus of this chapter is not on where be come from but the wonderful change that took place in his life when he meet Jesus!

The purpose of this book has been to study the evangelistic beginnings of individuals who were influenced by a single person to them making a decision to follow God or the Christ. In a lengthy study of the Apostles of Jesus, I like most have come to many a death-end when trying to find out information about Simon. One of the last mentioned, Simon has a very small profile in the Gospels and about all we know about him is the listings of his name among Jesus disciples in Matthew, Mark, Luke and Acts 1:13. Granted, any time the disciples are mentioned in the Gospel stories we can conclude that Simon was there, but with many of the disciples of Jesus actually individual stories about them are mentioned but with Simon none are mentioned. But with the other disciples whose stories are clearly explained, I have come to the verdict that if Jesus led Peter, Andrew, James, John, Philip, and Nathaniel to Himself so He also found Simon. My deduction is this: when Simon was called to be an apostle he was already a believer!

Simon, the other Simon of the Apostle Band, was an extremist: "Simon called Zelotes"! (Luke 6:15 and Acts 1:13) Today Simon would be called a revolutionary or maybe even a terrorist. During the days of Jesus there were a number of political and religious extremist groups operating in the region. We are familiar with the Pharisees and the Sadducees (Matthew 3:17), but less know were the Herodians (Mark 3:6) and the Zelotes. I have come to the belief that Simon was a lover of his land and the occupation by the Romans was heavy on his heart. The group that he seemingly was associated with had a long history of resisting those that would take the Promised Land away from the Jews. The cause he followed could be traced back a few hundred years when after the Babylonian Captivity and the return of the Israelites to their homeland a series of invaders always seemed to have control of the land, that was until the Maccabees came along. I have come to believe that the Zelotes came out of that movement when a father and five of his sons regained control of Palestine for a short time. The father of the Maccabees was reported to have said on his death bed: "and now my children **be zealous** for the law and give your lives for the covenant of your father'! (Apocrypha-I Maccabees 2:50) Hence the term and title 'Zelotes'; was Simon the Canaanite a Zelote?

This group became the most violent of all the political groups and some scholars even believe that Barabbas might have been a Zelote (Mark 15:7) and the assassins of Acts 21:38 might have been Zelotes. A passionate patriot who might have thought that the only way to get out from under the control of the Romans was by armed revolt; that is until he met Jesus. If anyone was out of place in the apostle group it must have been Simon, and yet Jesus picked him. What was it about Simon that Jesus liked? I believe the answer is found in one of the most controversial stories in the Life of the Christ, the event that resulted in Jesus cleaning out the Temple. John would record this after the stocking event: "And his disciples remembered that it was written, ***The zeal of thine house hath eaten me up.***" (John 2:17) I believe Jesus was attracted to Simon because they both were zealous people. Perhaps, that was the reason the Canaanite started listening to a carpenter from Galilee? I believe at that beginning the only difference was Jesus' zeal was under control but Simon's zeal was unbridled. We have a lot of zealous fundamentalist today out of control. I also have come to believe that John the Baptist was a Zelote: "He was a burning and a shining light: and ye were willing for a season to rejoice in his light." (John 5:35) That was Jesus' description of John the Baptist. I think Jesus saw John the Baptist, not as a political freedom fighter, but a spiritual freedom fighter.

I feel this is why Jesus called Simon, for He believed all He had to do was redirect that zeal in the right direction, and I believe that is exactly what He did. Simon started out a Zelote for a political movement, but became a Zelote for a new faith movement and with him and his other apostles they would as the world would one day note: "And when they found them not, they drew Jason and certain brethren unto the rulers of the city, crying, *These that have turned the world upside down* are come hither also." (Acts 17:6) From an extremist to an evangelist is how I describe the change in Simon in my study of The Twelve Apostles: from political ambitions to peaceful aspiration; what a transformation from a military metabolism to a missionary's mind. An ancient proverb goes something like this: **"Zeal is fit only for wise men but is found mostly in fools!"** I think Simon started this way, but Jesus turned him into a wise steward. Paul, another Zelote, maybe not in the organization but in his temperament and fixation on destroying the Church would write: "But *it is* good to be zealously affected always in *a good thing*, and not only when I am present with you." (Galatians 4:18) The word 'zealously' is from the root word 'zeo' which means to burn, or to be hot: literally to boil, but a controlled boil. We have a lot of boiling mad Christians today but most of them are out of control. Stilson Hutchins says: "There is no zeal as intemperate and cruel as that which is backed by ignorance!" How we need to be as Paul spoke of God's angels in Hebrews: "And of the angels he saith, who maketh his angels spirits, and his ministers a flame of fire." (Hebrews 1:7) I found this poem years ago and I still like it: "Set us afire Lord, stir us to pray, while the world perishes we go on our way, purposeless, passionless, day after day, set us afire Lord, stir us to pray." I believe that's explains the change that took place tine Simon's life when he meet Jesus at an unnamed time, in an unknown place, and in an unnoticed encounter! Have you had such a meeting yet?

James M. Mason writes: "A zealous soul without meekness is like a ship in a storm, in danger of wrecks. A meek soul without zeal is like a ship in a calm that moves not as fast as it ought!" Simon at first was like that first ship, and most of us are like the last ship. We both needed Jesus to show us the right kind of zeal. Christ-like zeal is like what Julius Bate once said: "Zeal without knowledge is like fire without a grate to contain it; like a sword without a hilt to wield it by; like a high-bred horse without a bridle to guide it. It speaks without thinking, acts without planning, and seeks to accomplish a good end without the adoption of becoming mean!" When Jesus won over Simon, the Christ become Simon's grate, hilt, and bridle! "And whatsoever ye do, do *it* heartily, as to the Lord, and not unto men!" (Colossians 3:23) How would you define your zeal?

# 39

## WON: ZELEK THE AMMONITE
## BY: I Chronicles 11:39

Zelek the Ammonite, Naharai the Berothite, the armourbearer of Joab the son of Zeruiah.

## ONE: DAVID

WHILE DAVID WAS AT the Cave Adullam, he began to gather around him a group of exceptional warriors (I Samuel 22:1–2). Then when Ziklag became his home away from home (Bethlehem) another group of courageous soldiers became a part of his small personal army (I Chronicles 12:1–7). Out of these men-of-war came David's intriguing list of 'mighty men' (II Samuel 23:8). These were the men Jehovah built up to eventually make David king at Hebron and then a few years later at Jerusalem (I Chronicles 11:4–10). In the battles that they fought together that brought this story to God's appointed end, an elite group known as 'the thirty mighty men' (II Samuel 23:23) emerged as David's bravest of the brave, David's heroes of heroes, David's elite. As we have discovered, recorded in the Bible are actually two lists of these amazing warriors together with their genealogy or place of origin. In II Samuel 23:8–38 we have 37 soldiers listed (II Samuel 23:39) while in I Chronicles 11:11–47 there are an additional 16 who came from territories conquered by David's armies. David seemed to be no respecter of persons or race when it came to the makeup of his soldiers (God-like Acts 10:35). David also seemed to have that rare gift (like with the famous Carthaginian general Hannibal) of being able to muster loyalty from a variety of nationalities once hostile to the country of Israel and the people of the Jews. Hannibal, the greatest general of his time and always found on history's top warrior's list of all time, merged together an army that constantly beat the Roman Army with mercenaries that were African, Spanish, and Celtic. Unlike the Romans, Hannibal's forces were not heterogeneous in organization or armament and their quality depended entirely on their own leaders and the general in overall command, of which Hannibal was one of the best in the world, if not the best, but I believe the world has overlooked the genius of David in this ability. When you consider what David did, though his armies were as large as Hannibal's, the men he was able to melt together became exceptional in their warfare with David!

In my compiling of a combined list of David's 'mighty men', I have come to a soldier whose only distinction in this famous brotherhood is his race, and I believe eventually his conversion. He was Zelek the Ammonite, whose name means 'split' or 'rent'! Perhaps, the only way we can understand fully how amazing it was to have such a man like Zelek in David's Army, we must first share a brief history of the Ammonites written by Robert Young: "Ammon-a fellow-countryman. The name of the descendants of Ben-Ammi, the younger son of Lot by his youngest daughter born in a cave of a mountain near Zoar..... Genesis 19:30–38. Their country lay at the northeast of Moab, and east of the tribes of Reuben, between the Arnon and the Jabbok Rivers. Their border was strong (Numbers 21:24); they were not distressed or meddled with by Israel; the original inhabitants of their country were the giants, and called Zamzummim (great and tall, and many as the Anakim), who were destroyed by the Ammonites (Deuteronomy 2:19, 20, 37); their chief city was Rabbath-Ammon, and it contained the gigantic bedstead of Og, King of Bashan (Deuteronomy 3:11)....none of their nation was to be allowed to enter the congregation of Jehovah to the tenth generation (Deuteronomy 23:3)..... They along with Amalek, joined Eglon, King of Moab, B. C. 1354, and smote Israel, and took Jericho, the city of the palm-trees (Judges 3:13); their gods were served by the children of Israel, B. C. 1161, so that Jehovah sold the latter into their hands, and they served them 18 years, on both sides of the Jordan. Israel crying to Jehovah, the Ammonites encamped in Gilead, but were defeated by Jephthah, who drove them from Aroer to Minnith (Judges 10:6–8, 11:1–33); their chief national god was Chemosh (Judges 11:24); they besieged Jabesh-Gilead, when Nahash their king threatened its inhabitants with a severe penalty, but he was discomfited by King Saul (I Samuel 11:1–11; 12:12); they were accordingly vexed by Saul thereafter (I Samuel 14:47); their silver and gold taken in battle were dedicated to Jehovah by David (II Samuel 8:12; I Chronicles 18:11); Hanun their king, the son of Nahash, having insulted the messengers of David, hired the Syrians to help him, but they were defeated by Joab and Ahishai (II Samuel 10:1-19); I Chronicles 19:1-9); who also besieged Rabbah his capital, and took it, whereon David went to complete the capture, and took all the spoil, and humbled the inhabitants (II Samuel 11:1, 12; I Chronicles 20:1-3)." And out of this history came a warrior by the name of Zelek!

How does a man change sides after such a history of hostility? How does a citizen of one race switch his allegiance to another race? How does an archenemy flip to the side of an archenemy and become one of its kings greatest soldiers? Remember, we have already studied a Philistine (see chapter #6) that switched sides, those that became David's personal guard, but there was a group of them; well over six hundred, but Zelek was alone! The only other Ammonite I could find in the Bible that was friendly towards David was a man named Shobi, the son of Nahash, the brother of Hanun, of the city of Rabbah, who took supplies to support David at Mahanaim when David was fleeing from the Absalom rebellion (II Samuel 17:27). All other relationships between the Ammonites and the Israelites are negative in the Scriptures. Solomon would marry an Ammonite, not doubt a political marriage as were so many of Solomon's marriages. Naamah would give birth to Rehoboam, the next king of Israel and the king that would split Israel into two nations (I Kings 14:21, 31; II Chronicles 12:13). Naamah was also one of Solomon's wives that turned his heart away from God in his older years (I Kings 11:1, 5, 7, 33). So there is quite a history between the Ammonites and the Israelites, and yet I come back to our hero Zelek. How does a single Ammonite knowing the history between these two races end up on a list of David's 'mighty men'?

So I ask you again, how does a man that worships the wrong god (Judges 11:24), from an incestuous beginning (Genesis 19:35), from a cursed nation (Genesis 12:3), from a hater of Israel end up a celebrated soldier in David's divisions? I could come up with only one answer. A number of years ago after reading Elizabeth Elliot's 1956 book "Through Gates of Splendor" about her husband's death with his four friends at the hands of the Auca people, and the reason that these five young Americans even went into the Amazon rain forest: ". . ..and hath redeemed us to God by Thy blood out over EVERY kindred. . ...and nation." (Revelation 5:9) They went so that a representative from the Auca people would be at the throne. I am convinced now that the Ammonites also needed a representative and I am persuaded his name is Zelek. So God reached down His hand and 'rent' an individual from the nation of Ammon to be present at His throne on that day!

Revelation 7:9–10-". . .and lo, a great multitude, which no man could number, of all nations (including Ammon), and kindreds, and people, and tongues, stood before the throne. . .Salvation to our God which sitteth upon the throne, and unto the Lamb."

# 40

## WON: THE CANAANITE WOMAN
## BY: Matthew 15:22

And, behold, a woman of Canaan came out of the same coasts, and cried unto him, saying, Have mercy on me, O Lord, *thou* Son of David; my daughter is grievously vexed with a devil.

## ONE: JESUS

SOMEONE HAS DEFINED MERCY as "that action of God by which He withholds deserved penalty and alleviates suffering and distress!" The Psalmist wrote of God: "The Lord *is* **merciful** and gracious, slow to anger, and **plenteous in mercy**." (Psalm 103:8) In the life of a single Canaanite woman the depth of this kind of mercy can be clearly seen when the Christ came into her life. To those of us who heard her cry for 'mercy' since childhood and have known of her act of faith since boyhood, we know this plea has echoed down through the ages as the Gentile's cry for mercy from a Hebrew God. Cornelius (Acts 10) the Roman centurion from Caesarea has gotten all the press and recognition over the years for being the first Gentile to be converted, but for me this Canaanite woman was the one that revealed Christ's purpose to administer mercy to the Gentiles as well as the Jews: "Behold my servant, whom I have chosen; my beloved, in whom my soul is well pleased: I will put my spirit upon him, and he shall shew judgment to the Gentiles." (Matthew 12:18) This was actually a quote from Isaiah 42:1 and so again we can see in our story the 'won by one' concept as seen in the healing of her daughter!

After having been rejected by the leaders of his own people (Matthew 15:1–20): "He came unto his own, and his own received him not." (John 1:11) Jesus leaves Galilee for a short trip into the region of Tyre and Sidon. We would call this area southern Lebanon today. Mark's version of the story says this: "The woman was a Greek, a Syrophenician by nation; and she besought him that he would cast forth the devil out of her daughter." (Mark 7:26) Canaanite, Sidonian, Phoenician, Greek, or Syrian, which? Probably all of the above! The area witnessed many conquerors over the years, so the people of Jesus' day were a mixed breed of Gentile nations, mostly wicked and very ungodly. Matthew seems to concentrate on her Canaanite roots, a much despised nation in the Bible; sinners beyond measure, but not beyond mercy! Their worship of the abominable Moloch, Astarte, and Baal had brought them under divine condemnation and judgment of the Almighty. However, the Israelites failed to execute God's commandments (Deuteronomy 7:1–3), opening a door of mercy for at least one Canaanite and her family. Like Rahab the Amorite, this Canaanite simply called out for mercy and though her faith was tempted her perseverance paid off for her and her daughter. I again like the Psalmist on this: "Return, O Lord, deliver my soul: oh save me for thy mercies' sake." (Psalm 6:4) Mercy wins again, and this 'One' was 'Won' by Jesus' mercifulness. Amen and Amen!

I have come to the belief that Jesus had actually gone to the region for a rest (Mark 6:31-" And he said unto them, Come ye yourselves apart into a desert place, and rest a while: for there were many coming and going, and they had no leisure so much as to eat.") as He often did after a very long and tiring period of ministry. His grueling schedule often forced him into period of relaxation; another example of the humanity of the Saviour. We know his fame had reached this area (Matthew 14:24) because at this time Syria dominated the region. Though maybe unrecognized, He wasn't unknown! How this mother found Jesus isn't clear, but why she sought Him is very clear. A demon possessed daughter was a heavy burden, and is there any distance or obstacle a mother won't go to help her child? I find this story similar to the father who sought help for his demonic son (read Matthew 17:14–15), the genders are the only difference. In both cases Jesus was the answer, as it is today. Christ is still merciful to miserable parents with difficult children: "But Jesus said, Suffer little children, and forbid them not, to come unto me: for of such is the kingdom of heaven." (Matthew 19:14) Do you have one?

However, at first it would appear that Jesus would send this lady away (Matthew 15:23). In this initial rejection, there is a lesson to be learned about mercy. Mercy isn't something you get without much perseverance, but this Canaanite had plenty of that! When she couldn't get anything out of Christ, she haunted his disciples; reminding me of the widow of Jesus parable (Luke 18:1–8). This mother didn't care who healed her daughter, for it seemed she knew that Jesus had given His disciples the power of healing (Matthew 10:1–4). Soon the disciples, remember there were twelve at this time, came to Jesus for relief from her. Her harassment was rewarded, but again Jesus rejected her (Matthew 15:24), but once again she cried: "Lord, help me!" (Matthew 15:25) But again Jesus drives her away calling her a 'dog'! (Matthew 15:26) Her reply finally touched the heart of Jesus: "And she said, Truth, Lord: yet the dogs eat of the crumbs which fall from their masters' table." (Matthew 15:27) It was enough. The test was over. Her sterling faith had won in the end: "Then Jesus answered and said unto her, O woman, **great is thy faith**: be it unto thee even as thou wilt. And her daughter was made whole from that very hour." (Matthew 15:28) How often people miss Christ's mercy because they don't approach Him with genuine faith? Mercy is a precious virtue that God only gives out to those who sincerely want it. Jesus saw beyond the daughter's needs, remember a healing was simple to the Christ, but to heal the soul is another matter, for therein lies the greater miracle of this story, for like the woman at the well (John 4:3) I believe Jesus had also gone to the region to find a woman of faith-read again Acts 10:35!

So what are the qualities that bring mercy out? First, **there has to be worship.** (Matthew 15:25) Three times this woman address Jesus as Lord (Matthew 15:22, 25, 27). Until we see the Christ for who He really is mercy can't really be received. Second, **there has to be humility.** (Matthew 15:27) Instead of being insulted by what Jesus said to her, the mother humbled herself even further. So many like Naaman (II Kings 5) reject Jesus at first because they are not willing to humble themselves before Him. One must be humble to receive mercy. (James 4:6) Third, **there has to be faith.** (Matthew 15:28) Paul writes: "But without faith *it is* impossible to please *him*: for he that cometh to God must believe that he is, and *that* he is a rewarder of them that diligently seek him." (Hebrews 11:6) Is not this the testimony of this Canaanite? I believe this mother meet and adhered to all these three precepts, so is not this the reason she received mercy for herself and her child? In Edith Deen's book "Wisdom from Women of the Bible" she concludes her remarks on the Canaanite woman with these timely observations: "Each of us should ask ourselves how merciful we are to those with heartbreaking afflictions. If we communicate to them a spirit of love and mercy we can help a little. (Psalm 23:6-"Surely goodness and mercy shall follow me all the days of my life: and I will dwell in the house of the LORD for ever.") In His efforts among the poor, the needy, and the afflicted, Jesus proved that God's mercy seeks a higher good than the temporary relief of distress. Mercy signifies love to one another, the kind of love Jesus showed this grieving mother." Won by One!

# 41

## WON: ITHMAH THE MOABITE
## BY: I Chronicles 11:46

Eliel the Mahavite, and Jeribai, and Joshaviah, the sons of Elnaam, and Ithmah the Moabite.

## ONE: DAVID

WHO OF US HAS not studied the exemplary life of Ruth the Moabite (see chapter #15)? Who of us has not admired the tremendous faith it took for Ruth to follow her mother-in-law back to Bethlehem? Who of us has not read the story of Ruth and held our breath: would she or wouldn't she be Boaz's bride? Ruth has gone down in Hebrew history as one of the great proselytes to Judaism, and even entering the Messianic Line (Matthew 1:5). I have come to believe in my study of David's 'mighty men', another Moabite is worthy of our attention and study: Ithmah; another won by one candidate for our book!

The first thing we need to record is the ever growing list of foreign mercenaries that are numbered among David's elite troopers. Remember these famous warriors:

1. Ittai the Gittite-II Samuel 18:2-the soldier from Gath, a Philistine. (chapter #6)

2. Zelek the Ammonite-I Chronicles 11:39, a race from Lot's incest. (chapter #39)

3. Uriah the Hittite-II Samuel 23:39, a race that was condemned also. (chapter #33)

4. Ithmah the Moabite-I Chronicles 11:46, another race from Lot's incest.

The only other information we can glean from the Scriptures about Ithmah is the meaning of his name: purity. How does a man from a cursed race ("An Ammonite or Moabite shall not enter into the congregation of the Lord; even to their tenth generation shall they not enter into the congregation of the Lord forever." Deuteronomy 23:3) get pure? I feel like Ruth before him, Ithmah came into contact through his relationship with David with the Purifier: "And He shall sit as a Refiner and Purifier of silver: and He shall purify the sons of Levi, and purge them as gold and silver. . .." (Malachi 3:3) I have come to believe that as Peter would finally understand through his vision in Acts 10, that "of a truth I perceive that God is no respecter of persons (Ithmah): but in every nation (Moab) he that feareth Him, and worketh righteousness, is accepted with Him." (Acts 10:34–35)

I found this poem by an unknown author a number of years ago, and for me it speaks volumes about the meaning of Ithmah's name and its connection to Jesus Christ and us:

> He sat by a fire of seven-fold heat,
> As He watched by the precious ore,
> And closer He bent with a searching gaze
> As He heated it more and more.
> He knew He had ore that could stand the test,
> And He wanted the finest gold
> To mount as a crown for the king to wear,
> Set with gems with a price untold.
> So He laid our gold in the burning fire,
> Though we fain would have said Him, "Nay,"
> And He watched the dross that we had not seen,
> And it melted and passed away.
> And the gold grew brighter and yet more bright,
> But our eyes were to dim with tears,
> We saw but the fire-not the Master's hand,
> And questioned with anxious fears.
> Yet our gold shone out with a richer glow,
> As it mirrored a Form above,
> That bent over the fire, though unseen by us,
> With a look of ineffable love.
> Can we think that it pleases His loving heart
> To cause us a moment's pain?

Ah, No! but He saw through the present cross
The bliss of eternal gain.
So He waits thee with a watchful eye,
With a love that is strong and sure,
And His gold did not suffer a bit more heat,
Than was needed to make it pure.

Ithmah was a jewel set in refined gold in the crown of David's 'mighty men. Unlike the men of Judah or any other tribe of Israel, Ithmah was a traitor to his race and nation when he joined the army of their enemy. Like Ruth, only a spiritual conversion could have motivated such a revolt against home and homeland. Ithmah found faith in David's God I believe, and was numbered among David's famous soldiers, and God's 'won by one'.

Isaiah wrote this in his classic book: "And I will turn my hand upon thee, and purely purge away thy dross, and take away all thy tin." (Isaiah 1:25) As New Testament saints, Christ's work in us has a similar theme according to Peter: "That the trial of your faith being much more precious than of gold that perisheth, though it be tried with fire, might be found unto praise and honor and glory at the appearing of Jesus Christ." (I Peter 1:7) As saints of God, we will often endure the fires of sickness, suffering, and sever pain that the impurities of our lives might be purged away. These trials will not be pleasant, but the Purifier knows that they are necessary, and He will only make the process as hot as it necessary to get the cleansing done; the dross out, and the purest product refined! Jesus would teach in his classic Sermon on the Mount: "Blessed are the pure in heart; for they shall see God." (Matthew 5:8) Oswald Chambers writes on this concept: "We have to grow in purity. God makes us pure by His sovereign grace, but we have something to look after, this bodily life which we come in contact with other people." Life itself is a purifier, but it is used by the Master Purifier to make us "...conformed to the image of His Son." (Romans 8:29) That kind of purity takes a lot of purging and refining!

Let us today allow the Purifier to turn up the heat on our lives, so that in the end we will come forth as gold! A young man on my hall in college, Ron Hamilton, wrote this grand song after losing an eye: "God never moves without purpose or plan, when trying his servant and molding a man. Give thanks to the Lord though your testing's seems long; in darkness He giveth a song. I could not see through the shadow ahead; so I looked at the cross of my Saviour instead. I bowed to the will of the Master that day; then peace came and tears fled away. Now I can see testing comes from above; God strengthens His children and purges with love. My Father knows best, and I trust in His care; through purging more fruit I will bear. O rejoice in the Lord, He makes no mistakes. He knoweth the end of each path that I take. For when I am tried and purified, I shall come forth as gold!" I believe Ithmah was a product of this process, but have you been? Paul wrote: ". . .but be thou an example of the believers. . .in purity." (I Timothy 4:12)

# 42

## WON: MNASON THE CYPRIOTE
## BY: Acts 21:16

There went with us also *certain* of the disciples of Caesarea, and brought with them one Mnason of Cyprus, an old disciple, with whom we should lodge.

## ONE: BARNABAS

TODAY IN OUR "WON by One" series of devotionals on the famous Biblical stories about conversion, we stop to take notice of a Scriptural character that appears and disappears in one simple verse of Luke's history of the early Church; one of a multitude of unknown but not unnamed individuals recorded in Holy Writ. I decided to wrote on Mnason, not because we know a lot about him, but because he was from the island of Cyprus, one of the first areas the early Church evangelized, and because one of the purposes of this book is to number as many people groups (Revelation 5:9, 7:9) mentioned in the Bible that came to a saving knowledge of God, and who brought that individual to that conversion!

There is very little Biblical history in the Old Testament about Cyprus. Most feel that "Elishah" in Ezekiel 27:7 is speaking about the Island of Cyprus? Cyprus was known in ancient times as the land that traded mostly in blue and purple cloth. Because of its location in the Eastern Mediterranean, it more often than not had a foreign ruler governing it. The Phoenicians settled and ruled the island first because it was an important stopping off place for their sea-trade with far off and distant places. But in time the Syrians and then the Greek and then the Egyptians and then the Persians controlled this strategic island, one by one until by the time of our story the Romans were in control. In 58 BC, the Romans made it one of their provinces. So a Cypriote was a mixed race of people that had formed a unique people-group over the centuries before the arrival of the Christ (Galatians 4:4), but like all groups, they needed salvation, too!

Luke starts our look into the conversion of Mnason with these words: "Now they which were scattered abroad upon the persecution that arose about Stephen travelled as far as Phenice, and **Cyprus**, and Antioch, preaching the word to none but unto the Jews only. And some of them were men of **Cyprus** and Cyrene, which, when they were come to Antioch, spake unto the Grecians, preaching the Lord Jesus." (Acts 11:19-20) This is a little preached precept today, but I have become a believer in the truth that God allowed the early persecution of the Church so that the Gospel would be spread! I believe the early disciples and apostles had gotten stuck in Jerusalem and Judea and were slow in following Jesus exact instruction: "But ye shall receive power, after that the Holy Ghost is come upon you: and ye shall be witnesses unto me both in Jerusalem, and in all Judaea, and in Samaria, and unto the uttermost part of the earth." (Acts 1:8) Until the persecution started with Stephen began there was no Gospel witness in Samaria and the 'uttermost' including Cyprus. Again it is the Blood of the Martyrs that has more often than note sent the Church out evangelizing. Take for an example the five young martyrs of Ecuador in 1956; martyrdom has always sent the Church beyond to reach men like Mnason.

Mnason's only call to fame is that he was 'an old disciple'. Was he one of those original believers on the Island of Cyprus, or did he come along a bit later when the church at Antioch sent out the first recognized Gospel team in Barnabas, Saul, and Mark? "So they, being sent forth by the Holy Ghost, departed unto Seleucia; and from thence they sailed to Cyprus . . ." (Acts 13:4) Certainly the most famous Cypriote in the early Church was Barnabas himself: "And Joses, who by the apostles was surnamed Barnabas, (which is, being interpreted, The son of consolation,) a Levite, *and* of the country of Cyprus, having land, sold *it*, and brought the money, and laid *it* at the apostles' feet." (Acts 4:36-37) Barnabas came to the Lord long before the Stephen Persecution, so he isn't among those that are mentioned in Acts 11, yet it is Barnabas that leads a mission trip back to his home island (Acts 13:2). So is Barnabas the one that lead Mnason to the Christ? Barnabas is a great example of the instruction Jesus gave to the demonic of Gadarenes: "Howbeit Jesus suffered him not, but saith unto him, Go home to thy friends, and tell them how great things the Lord hath done for thee, and hath had compassion on thee." (Mark 5:19) To highlight and underline this concept by Christ I give you this story by Lettic M. Rae: "In November, 1940, while travelling from the Friendly Islands to British Guiana, the S.S. Rangitane was shelled and sunk by a German raider. After their capture, the crew was put ashore on the cannibal island of Emirau: a beautiful but malaria haunted islet where it was the intention of their captors all should perish. Once on the island the group knew they had to obtain food, but were afraid of the natives. Eventually, their hunger got the best of them and they cautiously made their way to the nearest village. The picturesque village hidden beneath dense tropical vegetation was quiet, empty, and deserted. Drawing near they head the sound of a voice singing in an English tongue: 'Jesus loves me this I know, for the Bible tells me so!' How assuring were those words. They entered the hut unafraid. It was a village church. A tall, fine-looking Solomon Islander with hawk-like features was conducting the service...He was the son of cannibal parents of the Solomon Islands, but, coming under the influence of western missionaries had become a Christian and had been sent to Fiji to be educated as a catechumen. When his training was complete his desire had been to go back to Emirau, which no missionary had yet visited, and where the people were savage cannibals, but eventually through his labors many had become converted and had been baptized during his years there. His first words to the castaways were: 'I think no cannibals now. I think all friendly!' With these words he took up his guitar, twanged the strings and sang sweetly and tunefully the beautiful chorus: 'I will make you fishers of men if you follow me!'" That boat load of passengers were saved from almost certain death because a believer went back to evangelize his own people, just like Barnabas!

As with many of our conversion stories, can we be certain who was the actual individual that God used to being them to Himself, No! But what we know is Mnason is a wonderful example of the individual who was gloriously saved sometime in his past, so that when Paul and Luke were returning to Jerusalem through Caesarea that this old believer was added to Luke's account because of the hospitality he showed them. So whether or not Mnason was a co-disciple with Barnabas in those early days when the Gospel was spread by unrecorded Christians, or he was a product of the migration of the early disciples after Stephen's death, or a convert from Barnabas and Paul's missionary trip to the island, I know not, only the Good Lord knows (Acts 2:47), but this I know: it is very important that we go back home for men like Mnason. I think you know this about Barnabas and the reason I give him the credit for this conversion is his love for Cyprus and the Cypriotes. Even after Barnabas' split with Paul it says: "And the contention was so sharp between them, that they departed asunder one from the other: and so Barnabas took Mark, and sailed unto Cyprus." (Acts 15:39) Barnabas was seeking Cypriotes!

# 43

**WON**: ISMAIAH THE GIBEONITE
**BY**: I Chronicles 12:4

And Ismaiah the Gibeonite, a mighty man among the thirty, and over the thirty; and Jeremiah, and Jahaziel, and Johanan, and Josabad the Gederathite.

**ONE**: DAVID

A<small>FTER</small> D<small>AVID</small> <small>FLED</small> <small>FROM</small> King Saul in his early twenties, he began to assemble a mercenary army around him of 'mighty men of valor' who would eventually assist him in attaining the throne of Israel (I Chronicles 11:10). The first group joined David at the Cave of Adullam and was a force of ". . ..about four hundred men." (I Samuel 22:2) I have come to believe that these four hundred were actually an answer to David's prayer recorded in Psalm 142: "I looked on my right hand, and beheld, but there was no man that would know me; refuge failed me, no man cared for my soul." (Psalm 142:4) Like Elijah after him, David felt he was alone, just like Elijah felt he was alone, but neither was alone. Remember, Elijah had seven thousand friends (I Kings 19:18), and David's friends would soon number in the thousands as well! God had heard their supplications.

A number of years later David had moved out of Israel because the threat on his life had intensified with King Saul's passionate pursuit of his former armourbearer (I Samuel 16:21). David fled with his men to the king of Gath and became a mercenary captain for King Achish. (I Samuel 27) Hiring his men out to Achish resulted in the Philistine king giving David his own town; a place called Ziklag. It was to that place the second great group of men joined David's band (I Chronicles 12:1–2). By now David's force had group to over 600 (I Samuel 27:2). If we compare the two number: 400 at Adullam and now 600 at Ziklag, we come to the conclusion that I Chronicles 12 is giving us some of the names of the two hundred plus that come to David at Ziklag. The description of I Chronicles 12 starts with the Benjamin Band, and then the Gibeonite Group, and their commander Ismaiah will be our Won by One focus. Again I believe this leader and his men were in direct answer to David's appeal to God for helpers! (I Chronicles 12:18)

As we have shared many times throughout this expedition into won by one heroes and heroines of our book, David drew warriors to his side not only from the tribes of Israel, but from indigenous people groups from Canaan itself (see chapters 6, 33, 39, 41). Ismaiah was not a Benjamite, or even from David's tribe of Judah. The first thing mentioned about this 'mighty man' is his race: Gibeonite, or a resident of the Amorite city of Gibeon. It was Ismaiah's ancestors that had tricked Joshua into making an alliance with them in the early days of the war for the control of Canaan. These crafty people had survived annihilation by convincing Joshua that they actually lived in a far off and distant land (Joshua 9) when in reality they were just a few miles from Joshua's latest conquest: Ai! If the march of the Hebrews would have continued as God had originally planned the next city on Joshua's hit list was Gibeon. If that peace treaty hadn't been signed then Ismaiah would never have been born! In an amazing twist of God's providence, Ismaiah's forefathers lived to produce a soldier that would eventually help David attain what Joshua and his armies never did: the mastery of Canaan.

Though we have no knowledge of any of Ismaiah's military exploits, we are told that he was given command over a group called 'the thirty'. We have seen this number used before in a description of the first group of 'mighty men' (II Samuel 23:24). I have come to believe that 'the thirty' was a unit description, or a grouping of David's warriors that fought together. Maybe, a special force unit (I Chronicles 11:25) that was called on for dangerous missions when a small group was needed verses the entire army. Ismaiah was 'a mighty man among the thirty', and 'over the thirty'. David seemingly chose his 'mighty men' based on ability not race; skills not residence, and character not background. Men like Ismaiah should be an inspiration to us all. Despite his background (from a cursed race) and his birth certificate (born among slaves-Joshua 9:21), Ismaiah attained to a position of honor for himself and his race, by turning too and accepting God's man for the kingship of Israel. So too must we. We are born into a cursed race (John 8:44), and born into the depraved family of sinners (Ephesians 2:1). God sent His only begotten Son to be the captain of our salvation (Hebrews 2:10). Have you joined Jesus' band yet? Have you taken up arms against your old master? If like Ismaiah you switch side you too will one day be a part of the winning side!

I find it interesting that every time we begin another 'won by one' search the meaning of the name fits in nicely to the narrative of our spiritual thoughts. David's 'mighty men' were in direct results to intercession and supplication and Ismaiah means "The Lord Hears"! David would write in another psalm: "The Lord will hear when I call unto Him." (Psalm 4:3) I do not know when the Lord heard the heart cry of David for the first time, and I know not when the Almighty heard the heart cry of Ismaiah for the first time, but I believe there was a time like with me. Jew or Gentile it makes no difference because God is always listening for a genuine call, a soul's cry. We have highlighted before God's task as He gathers and gains a representative from very nation and race (Revelation 5:9 and 7:9). I don't know if Ismaiah was the first Gibeonite saved, just like I don't know if Ruth was the first Moabite saved, but this I know: it all started when a cry was made to a listening God. Because God never slumbers or sleeps, the cry will be heard. I love the story of Elijah on Mount Carmel when he gave the priests of Baal the first chance to stir their god into action. They cried and call for most of a day, but no response from the fire god of Canaan. Surely it would be easy for a fire god to give fire, but there was no reply to their prayers and supplications. (I Kings 18) It appeared that Baal couldn't hear.

Then it was Elijah's turn and after constructing the altar he made a short supplication and before he ended his prayer the fire fell (I Kings 18:36–38), why, because Elijah believed in the Lord that hears. Do you believe in such a God? Is that the reason Ismaiah's parents gave him the name they did? Had they converted first? If they did they were not the first to switch gods because of what Jehovah had done. Remember Rahab converted not because of the spies, but because of what she had heard about what Jehovah had done for the children of Israel (Joshua 2:8–11). I find it interesting that in many of the conversion stories of the Bible the one that converts, converts because of some attribute of God. The seeing God was the reason that Hagar converted (see chapter #25-Genesis 16:13). How many convert because the Almighty has a great ear? He is a great listener? I know it is so nice to know that when I open my heart that I know someone is listening to my plea, my concerns, my needs, and my feelings. As I rewrite this article I am watching my 39-years old son die of lung and liver cancer. It has been a comfort to know that I can share my heart concerns and my questions about this trial to 'a listening God'! Psalm 65:2: "O thou that hearest prayer, unto Thee shall all flesh come." Surely one of the aspects of 'won by one' is the reality that we serve a God who hears!

# 44

## WON: THE NINEVEHITE KING
## BY: Jonah 3:6

For word came unto the king of Nineveh, and he arose from his throne, and he laid his robe from him, and covered *him* with sackcloth, and sat in ashes.

## ONE: JONAH

IN THE GREAT EXPANSION of the world's first empire, Nimrod, 'the mighty hunter', (Genesis 10:8–10) is given credit for building the ancient city of Nineveh (Genesis 10:11). It would eventually become known as the capital of the mighty Assyrian Empire. Located in what we would call northern Iraq today, Nineveh would become one of the great cities of the ancient world. Biblically speaking, this infamously wicked city is not mentioned again until the days of the Hebrew prophet Jonah: "He restored the coast of Israel from the entering of Hamath unto the sea of the plain, according to the word of the Lord God of Israel, which he spake by the hand of his servant Jonah, the son of Amittai, the prophet, which *was* of Gathhepher." (II Kings 14:25) From that time onward Jonah and Nineveh would be linked because of God's command to the reluctant prophet to preach the coming demise of the city, but a king's repentance changed everything.

Historically, the king of Assyria was a man by the name of Pul (II Kings 15:19). This leads us to a question: was the king of Assyria the same as the king of Nineveh? With the political structure of that day probably not! The king of Nineveh, the focus of this chapter, was probably just a city-state king, not the king of the Assyrian Empire. A good case in point is when King Benhadad of Syria attacked King Ahab of Israel he come with 32 kings with him (I Kings 20:1). The Bible actually records many notable kings of Assyria: like Tiglathpileser (II Kings 15:29), Shalmanassar (II Kings 17:3), Sennacherib (II Kings 18:13), and Esarhaddon (II Kings 19:37). Eventually this wicked and murderous empire was taken over by King Nebuchadnezzar of Babylonian, but not before the greatest recorded revival in the ancient world among Gentiles happened, and not before one of the most amazing Won by One conversions took place. I am of course talking about the Nineveh revival and the greatest prize of all 'the king of Nineveh'!

As I read the story of this mighty revival, I see the king of Nineveh playing a big part in the turning of his citizens to the true and living God: "And he (the king) caused *it* to be proclaimed and published through Nineveh by the decree of the king and his nobles, saying, Let neither man nor beast, herd nor flock, taste any thing: let them not feed, nor drink water: but let man and beast be covered with sackcloth, and cry mightily unto God: yea, let them turn every one from his evil way, and from the violence that *is* in their hands. Who can tell *if* God will turn and repent, and turn away from his fierce anger that we perish not?" (Jonah 3:7-9) Most are familiar with the story of Jonah and the Ninevehites and the roundabout way the preacher eventually got to Nineveh. One of the aspects of the Old Testament that is often overlooked is the fact that God wasn't just about the converting of the Jew, but the Gentile also. How many of the Hebrew prophets were also prophets to other nations? Remember what God told Jeremiah: "Before I formed thee in the belly I knew thee; and before thou camest forth out of the womb I sanctified thee, *and* I ordained thee a prophet unto the nations." (Jeremiah 1:5) Jesus would say this of Jonah: "For as Jonas was a sign unto the Ninevites, so shall also the Son of man be to this generation." (Luke 11:30) Both prophets to the Gentiles!

Situated on the junction of the Zab and Tigris Rivers, Nineveh was one of the largest cities in the ancient world with a population of over 120,000 people (Jonah 4:11). What we have for the mission of Jonah would be like sending a single missionary to Mexico City or Tokyo today. God has always sent forth His messengers before a judgment, for was not Noah a preacher of righteousness as well as a boat builder? (II Peter 2:5) So we are not surprised by God's desire that "The Lord is not slack concerning his promise, as some men count slackness; but is longsuffering to us-ward, not willing that any should perish, but that all should come to repentance." (II Peter 3:9) But why was Jonah so reluctant to take the message to the people of Nineveh? I believe Jonah wanted to see the city judged, but Jonah also believed something else: "...Therefore I fled before unto Tarshish: for I knew that thou *art* a gracious God, and merciful, slow to anger, and of great kindness, and repentest thee of the evil." (Jonah 4:2) Revival was possible!!!!

I am of the belief that part of Jonah's problem was his hatred for what the Assyrians had done to his country in his lifetime. The Assyrians had attacked Israel and killed many and had taken others captive and Jonah couldn't understand why God wouldn't destroy them when He seemingly was intending to do so. Jonah knew there was one thing ("So the people of Nineveh believed God, and proclaimed a fast, and put on sackcloth, from **the greatest of them** even to the least of them.-Jonah 3:5) that would change the heart of God and when it happened Jonah was displeased (Jonah 4:1). Rare even according to the Bible, yet not without merit: "For ye see your calling, brethren, how that not many wise men after the flesh, not many mighty, not many noble, are called." (I Corinthians 1:26) It says 'not many', but it doesn't say 'not any', so the king of Nineveh was one of the 'noble' called! And what we have illustrated here is the four stages of revival:

1. It was because of the 'foolishness of preaching'! Compare I Corinthians 1:21 and Jonah 3:2) And it still is preaching, not singing, nor witnessing, but preaching!

2. It was the going of 'a preacher'! Compare Matthew 28:19, Romans 10:14 and Jonah 3:3). Go is still the first ingredient in the GOpel; why Jonah had to go!

3. It was the message of 'repentance' that caused the revival! Compare Matthew 3:2 and 4:17 and Jonah 3:4) Jesus told this was the message in Luke 44:47.

4. It was because of 'believing' in the message, or believing God that the people were saved from the judgment! Compare Acts 16:31 and Jonah 3:5 and it still is!

We often forget that God's requirements for conversion haven't changed from the day of the Ninevehite to this day: "If my people, which are called by my name, shall humble themselves, and pray, and seek my face, and turn from their wicked ways; then will I hear from heaven, and will forgive their sin, and will heal their land." (II Chronicles 7:14) And that 'my people' are not just the Jewish people but: "...God is no respecter of person: but in every nation he that feareth him, and worketh righteousness, is accepted with him." (Acts 10:34-35) So a careful reading of Jonah 3:5-10 will reveal this revival, like all revivals, happen because of God and not just because of the preacher; it's the message!

Today, the cities of the world still need evangelists, even reluctant ones, to proclaim repentance. Even the noble need to be told to repent, and though the response maybe just a few and even fewer 'kings', the message is still to be proclaimed: "How then shall they call on him in whom they have not believed? And how shall they believe in him of whom they have not heard? And how shall they hear without a preacher?" (Romans 10:14)

# 45

## WON: DEMETRIUS THE CHRISTIAN
## BY: III John 12

Demetrius hath good report of all *men*, and of the truth itself: yea, and we *also* bear record; and ye know that our record is true.

## ONE: JOHN

AMONG DISCIPLES THERE ARE disciples and then there are disciples! In John's short epistle to his beloved Gaius (III John 1), he mentions two other disciples by name: Diotrephes and Demetrius. Diotrephes was proud and loved '. . .to have the preeminence among. . .' (III John 9) the brethren; he was a troublemaker and a hindrance to the cause of Christ; not only among his fellow brethren, but to the entire world. John condemns Diotrephes in three different areas:

1. In the area of COMMUNICATION (III John 10) Diotrephes' testimony was one of 'prating': silly tattling with malicious words (Proverbs 10:8, 10).

2. In the area of CONTENTMENT (III John 10) Diotrephes' testimony was one of discontentment. Diotrephes was ambitious and dangerous (I Timothy 6:6).

3. In the area of COOPERATION (III John 10) Diotrephes' testimony was inhospitable. He even had the gall to refuse the last living apostle (John) to come and speak in the local church he belonged to (Romans 16:17). Wow, amazing!

After John's clear description of this disciple he gave Gaius this precept: "Beloved, follow not that which is evil, but that which is good. He that doeth good is of God: but he that doeth evil hath not seen God." (III John 11) I believe in order to reinforce this concept John introduces us to Demetrius; a disciple that was setting the proper standard and living an exemplary life as a true disciple of Jesus Christ. I am persuaded that the reason that Demetrius was chosen is that John knew this disciple because he had personally lead Demetrius to the Christ. John had written earlier in the epistle: "I have no greater joy than to hear that my children walk in truth." (III John 4) Demetrius was certainly walking in the truth (III John 12), so was Demetrius one of John's children in the faith? If someone thinks of a personal with 'a good report' will they think of you?

When Paul wrote his classic chapter on faith he wrote of the faithful and their faith with: "For by it the elders obtained *a good report*." (Hebrews 11:2) Paul would end his chapter with this: "And these all, having obtained *a good report* through faith, received not the promise." (Hebrews 11:39) Demetrius was also known for his 'good report'! What kind of a testimony do you have? Most simple strive to keep a good report among the brethren, but Demetrius was known for a good report among "all" men! This side of our testimony is often ignored; just as long we have a good report with God and our fellow Christians! Paul would write to the young believers at Thessalonica this: "That ye may walk honestly toward them that are without, and *that* ye may have lack of nothing." (I Thessalonians 4:12) Demetrius was a disciple that had just as good a testimony in the Church as outside the Church. I don't know if Demetrius was a minister, or would become a minister, but he certainly qualified in this category: "This *is* a true saying, If a man desire the office of a bishop; he desireth a good work... Moreover he must have *a good report* of them which are without; lest he fall into reproach and the snare of the devil." (I Timothy 3:1, 7) What kind of testimony do you have in the world; as one person asked another with this question: "Are you willing to put your testimony to the parrot test?" The parrot test you ask? Yes, the parrot test: would you be ashamed to sell the family parrot to the town gossip? Demetrius had no such fears, do you?

Not only was Demetrius remembered for his testimony in the world, but also for his testimony in the word 'of the truth itself'. It is one thing to have a good report with men but an entirely a different thing to have a good report with God who knows your thoughts and hidden actions. Enoch had such a report: "By faith Enoch was translated that he should not see death; and was not found, because God had translated him: for before his translation he had **this testimony**, that he pleased God." (Hebrews 11:5) I believe Demetrius had such a testimony as well, and that testimony had to do with the Christ because Jesus is the Truth: "Jesus saith unto him, I am the way, the truth, and the life: no man cometh unto the Father, but by me." (John 14:6) If you could see God's report card on you what would it reveal: Attitude-C+; Dedication-B-; Faithfulness-D+; Testimony-C; Service-F; and Spirituality-B+. Or would you have the report card that Demetrius had: straight A+? Paul would write to the believers in Philippi this: "Finally, brethren, whatsoever things are true, whatsoever things *are* honest, whatsoever things *are* just, whatsoever things *are* pure, whatsoever things *are* lovely, **whatsoever things are of good report**; if *there be* any virtue, and if *there be* any praise, think on these things." (Philippians 4:8) Is your life wrapped up in producing a good report like Demetrius? The Bible is clear on this and there is only one way to please God: "But without faith *it is* impossible to please *him*: for he that cometh to God must believe that he is, and *that* he is a rewarder of them that diligently seek him." (Hebrews 11:6) Amen and Amen!

Finally, not only did Demetrius have a good report in the world and in the Word, but also among his own brethren. Could you stand before your fellow-believers blameless? Paul challenged the Christians of Galatia with this: "As we have therefore opportunity, let us do good unto all *men*, **especially unto them who are of the household of faith**." (Galatians 6:10) There is a certain behaviour and standard that is expected of a true disciple of Christ no matter what the liberals in the faith and the moderates in the church may say. A disciple who has a good report among sinners and saints and His Saviour is a rare disciple today, but Demetrius was such a man in his day setting for us an example that we might also have such a testimony. Many years ago I found this poem by a man by the name of McDonald that I liked, and it goes like this: "Someday my candle will burn low, and flicker into night. Will there be then an afterglow to guide someone aright?" Demetrius had such an afterglow, and I believe this is what Jesus was talking about when He gave His disciple this challenge: "Ye have not chosen me, but I have chosen you, and ordained you, that ye should go and bring forth fruit, and *that* your fruit should remain. . ." (John 15:16) Jesus wanted His disciple to have a lasting testimony!

In John's third epistle he mentions three disciples: Gaius, Diotrephes, and Demetrius, each one only mentioned once in Scripture. Gaius was remembered as well-beloved (III John 1); Diotrephes (III John 9) was remembered for being notorious in his abuse and misuse of his spiritual position, but Demetrius (III John 12) was noteworthy for his exemplary example of a disciple with a good report among all men and God. That leaves me with the question of how we will be or are being evaluated. Who will we emulate, which life will we follow? Remember Paul wrote: "Be ye followers of me, even as I also *am* of Christ." (I Corinthians 11:1) I believe we ought to follow Demetrius. In the final analysis will our grade reflect more of a Diotrephes or a Demetrius? I pray we too will receive a good report and that our lives will reflect the image of our Lord Jesus Christ!

# 46

## WON: HIRAM THE PHOENICIAN
## BY: I Kings 5:7

And it came to pass, when Hiram heard the words of Solomon, that he rejoiced greatly, and said, Blessed *be* the LORD this day, which hath given unto David a wise son over this great people.

## ONE: DAVID

AS WITH PAUL IN the New Testament, I have come to the conclusion in this series of devotionals that David was what we have come to call a 'soul winner'. Maybe there were others like a Jonah that saw an entire city come to a knowledge of Jehovah, but in my research nobody seemed to point more people to God than David. In this series we have witnessed David's work among the Gittites (see chapter six), the Hittites (see chapter thirty-three), the Ammonites (see chapter thirty-nine), the Moabites (see chapter forty-one) and the Gibeonites (see chapter forty-three). In this chapter I would like to highlight and underlines David's influence on Hiram the king of Tyre, a Phoenician!

Located in what we would call modern Lebanon today, Tyre and Sidon were once the principle city-states of the mighty Phoenician Empire in the eastern Mediterranean. The Phoenicians were the first maritime power and their ships and merchants carried trade throughout the region even when they ceased being the political and military power in the Mediterranean basin. The Phoenicians were a Canaanite race with its primary political, economic and religious center being Tyre. Tyre was the capital of an extensive trading empire that stretched from Spain in the west to some say India to the east. A careful read of Ezekiel 27 will give you a grand description of the extent of the Phoenicians through the eyes of the Hebrew prophet. Interestingly, the Phoenician land was given to the tribe of Asher, but because they never allotted the land the Phoenicians, like the Philistines, were a constant thorn in their side, but not to the degree of the Philistines. As with the other people groups the Jew allowed to live, the door was open for the most famous Phoenician of the Bible to come to believe in the God of David!

"And Hiram king of Tyre sent messengers to David, and cedar trees, and carpenters, and masons: and they built David an house." (II Samuel 5:11) This is the first time Hiram's name is recorded in the Bible. Hiram was the first, or probably, the first foreign leader to recognize David's new kingdom. At this time Phoenician was a power in the region and for this recognition to come would legitimates David's place in the area. Because Phoenicia had a monopoly on the lumber and were well skilled in construction, it was to him David turned for the construction of his first palace in Jerusalem. Eventually this arrangement seemed to result in an alliance that lasted well beyond David's reign: "And Hiram king of Tyre sent his servants unto Solomon; for he had heard that they had anointed him king in the room of his father: **_for Hiram was ever a lover of David._**" (I Kings 5:1) As with his father before him, Hiram was the first to recognize the kingship of Solomon after David's death. Note in the verse Hiram's great love of David! Often loving friendship is an avenue the Holy Spirit uses to bring unbelievers to Christ. 'Friendship' evangelism has been a form of witnessing since the earliest days of Jesus' ministry. Think with me about how John and Andrew, Peter and Philip and Nathaniel came to Jesus-read John 1:35–51. Few speak of it because of James 4:4-"...whosoever therefore will be a friend of the world is the enemy of God." Granted, we are not to be friends with the world, but we can be friendly in the world. Friendliness will produce friends and friends can be brought to the Lord. I believe that is how David had such an influence on the pagan king from Tyre, the Phoenician Hiram.

Eventually Solomon and Hiram formed an alliance (I Kings 5:12) and even went into a maritime business together (I Kings 10:11, 22). The plans and materials for the great Temple project were laid out by David, but it was left to Solomon to actually build the House of God, but Hiram helped (I Kings 9:11). It was in connection to the building of the Temple that I have come to the belief that Hiram was a believer in Jehovah! For me the key phrase in the verse I printed at the beginning of this chapter is: ". . .blessed be the Lord this day. . ." This statement is a recognition of the God of David and the God of Solomon, and by now you know my chief argument for these Gentiles coming to know the Almighty was Peter's statement to the Gentile Cornelius in Acts 10:34-35: ". . .God is no respecter of persons: but in every nation he that feareth him, and worketh righteousness, is accepted with him." I have come to believe that Hiram was one of those 'persons'! Some would say that the building of the Temple was just a business deal with Hiram, but I would have you reread I Kings 5:7-12 and draw your own conclusions according to Romans 14:5, but as for me I see the Won by One precept again!

I have come to believe in my own mind that 'blessed be the Lord this day' was Hiram's statement of faith, and that faith is verified and fortified by a work of righteousness, the building of 'the House of God'. Remember the teachings of James: "Even so faith, if it hath not works, is dead, being alone. Yea, a man may say, Thou hast faith, and I have works: shew me thy faith without thy works, and I will shew thee my faith by my works." (James 2:17-18) Hiram didn't only supply the timber for the Temple; he also supplied the chief contractor for the project; another man by the name of Hiram (I Kings 7:13-14, 20). Reading the story can be confusing because of this but for me the truth remains. We often forget that the Temple wasn't to just be a worship place for the Jews, but for all nations and peoples according to Jesus Himself: "And he (Jesus) taught, saying unto them, Is it not written, **My house shall be called of all nations the house of prayer**? but ye have made it a den of thieves." (Mark 11:17) I have come to believe that the use of the two Hirams was no accident, for Jesus' great commission was already in effect in Jerusalem long before Pentecost through men like David and Solomon!

God's eternal plan of salvation has and continues to include the whole world: "And he is the propitiation for our sins: and not for ours only, but also for *the sins of* **the whole world.**" (I John 2:2) Just because not everybody will believe, or all Phoenicians will believe doesn't mean that some won't. And though we often think that world-wide evangelism started after the Holy Spirit fell at Pentecost, I have this final thought on the conversion of King Hiram and the after effects of that conversion. As I mentioned before Solomon and Hiram went into business together sending Phoenician sailing ship all over the then known world (I Kings 10:22). Besides being a business venture was this one of the first world-wide evangelistic outreaches? I believe the Jews sailors and Phoenician sailors who believed in Jehovah would have shared the truth about the

Almighty. I believe that the mariners of Hiram and Solomon might have been the first evangelists and missionaries to a lost and dying world, and only heaven knows, but I believe this. Was this an opportunity missed or an opportunity fulfilled? Only the throne of God will tell: "After this I beheld, and, lo, a great multitude, which no man could number, of all nations, and kindreds, and people, and tongues, stood before the throne." (Revelation 7:9)

# 47

## WON: ARISTARCHUS THE MACEDONIAN
## BY: Acts 19:29

And the whole city was filled with confusion: and having caught Gaius and Aristarchus, men of Macedonia, Paul's companions in travel, they rushed with one accord into the theatre.

## ONE: PAUL

IT WAS SOLOMON WHO gave us the great precept: "Where *there is* no vision, the people perish. . ." (Proverbs 29:18), but for me it was when Mrs. Charles E. Cowman wrote in her classic devotional "Springs in the Valley" that his precept was brought home to me. And I quote: "Faith must first have visions: faith sees a light, if you will, an imaginary light, and leaps! Faith is always born of vision and hope. We must have the gleam of the thing hoped for shining across the waste before we can have an energetic and energizing faith. Are we not safe in saying that the majority of people have no fine hopes, are devoid of the vision splendid, and therefore, have no spiritual audacity in spiritual adventure and enterprise? Our hopes are petty and peddling, and they don't give birth to crusades. There are no shining towers and minarets on our horizon, no new Jerusalem, and therefore we do not set out in chivalrous explorations. We need a transformation in 'the things hoped for'. We need to be renewed in the mind, and renewed in mind daily. We need to have the far-of towering summits of vast and noble possibilities enthroned in our imagination.

Our gray and uninviting horizons must glow with the unfading colors of immortal hopes." If Solomon gave it and Cowman explained it, then, it was 'the man from Macedonia' who illustrates it, remember: "And a vision appeared to Paul in the night; There stood a man of Macedonia, and prayed him, saying, Come over into Macedonia, and help us." (Acts 16:9) I am not saying Aristarchus was the man, but he could have?

It was the late great Robert Louis Stevenson that said: "No man is of any use until he has dared everything." Paul was such a man, but before he did he needed a vision, and so should we. **First, we must look for such a vision.** Paul was on his way through Asia Minor (modern Turkey) when he set his eyes southward and westward, but Luke explains: "Now when they had gone throughout Phrygia and the region of Galatia, and were forbidden of the Holy Ghost to preach the word in Asia." (Acts 16:6) Not know as one who waits, Paul pressed on and would have gone to Bithynia, but again Luke explains: "After they were come to Mysia, they assayed to go into Bithynia: but the Spirit suffered them not." (Acts 16:7) Having blocked by the Holy Spirit from going in three points of the compass Paul arrives in Troas not knowing where the Lord wanted him to go: "And they passing by Mysia came down to Troas." (Acts 16:8) S. D. Gordon writes on this: **"It's safe to trust God's methods, and to go by His clock!"** I remember a time when I had a desire to return and pastor my home church in Perham, Maine. The call seemed so clear to me, but when I was rejected by the congregation my desire was scattered and the direction I sought was closed. I needed a new vision, and I too had to wait like Paul for the Holy Spirit's leading. We like Paul must be patient to wait for God's vision and timing. Joseph must have wondered in the Egyptian prison why he had been forgotten by Pharaoh's butler after the fulfillment of his vision (Genesis 40:23). But in God's perfect timing Joseph was lifted up to the premiership; the prison kept in perspective the mission that would follow. Such was the case with Paul and Macedonia and a man named Aristarchus he would meet there. Someone once wrote: "There is simplicity about God in working out His plans, yet a resourcefulness equal to any difficulty, an unswerving faithfulness to His trusting child, and an unforgetting steadiness in holding to His purpose." Paul was destined for Macedonia and Aristarchus and all he needed were his marching orders from God to continue and the 'won by one' experience he would have when he got there.

**Second, we must wait for such a vision.** How long Paul waited in Troas Luke does not tell us, but we know that while he waited he witnessed where he was. He worked to spread the Gospel despite the uncertainty where he was heading next; so many of us in waiting for our vision waste valuable time and opportunities to do God's work while we are waiting our marching orders. I still remember the time between my first and second churches, a period of six months that I still preached where I could, and started a ministry that is still going on to this day. I am just a few weeks away from the 2022–2023 session of what I call 'Winter in the Word'. In that first session (1978–1979), I gathered a group of people for a weekly evening school. This year I will share my 50th topic (some years I did two topics) which will be a powerpoint presentation on "The Twelve Apostles" in my 43rd year. You never know what the Lord will have you do while your vision is coming. Before Ananias had his vision about the conversion of Paul and his mission (Acts 9:10) was he not faithfully serving the Lord in Damascus? Before Cornelius had his vision (Acts 10:3) or Peter had his vision (Acts 10:11) were they not both doing something like giving, praying, witnessing? I have found that most visions come to people already working, already involved in the work of the Lord. Could this be the reason you have not received a vision yet? Hudson Taylor was already laboring among the poor in England before the Almighty gave him a vision for the poor in China; a vision for the lost somewhere else comes to those who are laboring for the lost where they are!

**_Third, we must respond immediately to such a vision,_** no matter the outcome. Luke records, and I believe the 'us' of this verse is Paul, Silas, and Luke: "And after he had seen the vision, immediately **we** endeavoured to go into Macedonia, assuredly gathering that the Lord had called **us** for to preach the gospel unto them." (Acts 16:10) Once the vision is clear there is not time to waste because Aristarchus needs the Lord. I don't believe that when Paul was in the Philippian jail (Acts 16:23–24) that he questioned the vision! Think with me for just a moment on the immediate results of following that vision: imprisonment, physical suffering, humiliation, and probably more affliction than Luke recorded. I feel this is why many don't seek a vision for the lost: the cost! Did Paul misunderstand the vision? No, the vision was clear, and we know from our key verse that a man named Gaius and a man named Aristarchus were the result and what of Lydia and her household (Acts 16:15) and the Philippian jail and family (Acts 16:34) and the countless others saved on Paul's tour of Macedonia. A man by the name of Field's writes: "Things don't just happen to us who love God, they're planned by His own hand, then molded and shaped, and timed by His clock; things don't just happen, they're planned!" And sometimes that plan is 'won by one', for we are not told when Paul meet Aristarchus, but Aristarchus become one of Paul's disciples and that is enough evidence for me to conclude that it was Paul himself that lead Aristarchus to God's salvation.

Today, you might be like Paul being directed towards a vision by being shut-off, shut-down from where you would like to go. God keeps blocking your advance until you are boxed in with nowhere to go. Settle in, keep working, the vision is on the way!

# 48

## WON: THE RECHABITE FAMILY
## BY: Jeremiah 35:19

Therefore thus saith the LORD of hosts, the God of Israel; Jonadab the son of Rechab shall not want a man to stand before me for ever.

## ONE: ELIJAH

THERE IS A STORY told of a rider that was leading a hunting party in England when they approached a shut gate. At that gate was a young gate keeper, and when the lead rider demanded that the gate be opened the lad replied: "I'm sorry sir, " answered the boy, "for my father sent me to guard the gate least somebody hunt on his land!" "Do you know who I am?" demanded the man. "No, sir," replied the boy. "I am the Duke of Wellington (the general that beat Napoleon at Waterloo)," explained the horseman. The boy removed his hat, but did not open the gate. He explained, "If you are the Duke of Wellington you would never ask me to disobey my father's orders!" Slowly, the Duke took off his hat and smiled at the boy and said, "I honor the boy who is faithful to his duty." With that the Duke of Wellington turned around and led the hunting party in a different direction. We live in an age where faithfulness in the little things isn't as honorable as it used to be, and faithfulness passed down through generations is even a rarer virtue. That is why I need to introduce you to a man named Jehonadab, and his unique story of "Won By One".

Jonadab was also called Jehonadab in II Kings 10:15. Jehonadab was a Kenite (I Chronicles 2:56) whereby his connection to Moses' father-in-law Jethro, who was the priest of the Kenites (Exodus 3:1) from the tribe of Midian. Midian was one of the sons born to Abraham through his second wife Keturah (Genesis 25:1-2). So Jehonadab had spiritual roots clear back to the father of the faithful, Abram (Genesis 15:6). In other words Jehonadab came from the right stuff, and had a name. Solomon proclaims: "A *good* name *is* rather to be chosen than great riches, *and* loving favour rather than silver and gold." (Proverbs 22:1) Matthew Bilher once wrote: "Faith is a thread slender and frail. Easy to tear, yet it can lift the weight of a soul up from despair!" So it is with faithfulness. It only takes one act of faithlessness to destroy it, but if faith remains it has the power to hold generations together, as with the Rechabite family.

Jehonadab's one call to fame and faithfulness took place during the uprising in Israel against the wicked dynasty of King Ahab (I Kings 16-II Kings 10). The primary revolt was led by a warrior by the name of Jehu, a man that Elijah was supposed to anoint (I Kings 19:16-17), but was left to his successor Elisha (II Kings 9:1-13). It was during that rebellion that Jehonadab comes on the scene, and just as quickly leaves the Biblical story: when Jehonadab accompanies Jehu to Samaria (II Kings 10:15-17) to destroy the remaining members of King Ahab's family including the wicked queen-mother Jezebel (II Kings 10:30-37). Following this one mention in the Scriptural text, Jehonadab and his family disappears from the Bible until Jeremiah the Hebrew prophet lists them in his great prophecy to the heroes of the past. Can one act of faithfulness remain and be remembered centuries later? Certainly it can! Missionary Mel Ruther tells a story that took place during the Second World War in the Pacific Theater. The Japanese had taken a little girl from her mother in order to force the mother to tell were certain enemy soldiers who they were chasing had gone. The mother refused until the Japanese soldiers tied the little girl above an open fire and their swords proceeded to cut strand by strand from the rope holding the girl. As the rope got dangerously thin the mother realized that soon the rope could no longer hold her child and into the fire she would go. Finally the mother screamed out: "I will tell!" Mel Ruther picks up the story with these words: "Up until this time the little girl had not made a single sound, but as she heard her mother scream out, 'I will tell', she raised her tortured little face toward heaven and even though it was twisted in suffering, there was a beautiful radiance as she called out, 'Mummie, Mummie, don't tell them. Don't tell them. Jesus will take care of us!' At that very instant a P-40 fighter plane zoomed over from out of nowhere and sent the Japanese scampering for cover. Strange enough the Japanese never returned and the mother was able to deliver her little daughter from the flames!" Yes, just a little girl, but faithful and still remembered.

The prophet Jeremiah had been commissioned by the Lord to show forth the faithlessness of Israel. How better to expose faithlessness than by comparing it to faithfulness? It was then Jeremiah was given these instructions from the Lord: "The word which came unto Jeremiah from the Lord in the days of Jehoiakim the son of Josiah king of Judah, saying, go unto the house of the Rechabites, and speak unto them, and bring them into the house of the Lord, into one of the chambers, and give them wine to drink." (Jeremiah 35:1-2) The instructions were clear but the result was enlightening: "Then I took Jaazaniah the son of Jeremiah, the son of Habaziniah, and his brethren, and all his sons, and the whole house of the Rechabites; and I brought them into the house of the Lord, into the chamber of the sons of Hanan, the son of Igdaliah, a man of God, which *was* by the chamber of the princes, which *was* above the chamber of Maaseiah the son of Shallum, the keeper of the door: and I set before the sons of the house of the Rechabites pots full of wine, and cups, and I said unto them, Drink ye wine." (Jeremiah 35:3-5) What happened next makes the connection to Jehonadab and a sterling example of faithfulness: read Jeremiah 35:6-10. Over two hundred years had now passed!

The original Kenites had migrated to Palestine with the Israelites in the great Exodus (Judges 4:17). They had stayed in the land as nomads, keeping the traditions of their fathers, refusing to drink wine and refusing to settle down in any one area to raise crops. This had been going on for centuries (from the Exodus in 1406 BC by the time of Jeremiah and the Babylonian Captivity it was the year 586 BC) and still in the days of Jeremiah they were maintaining their faithfulness to the instructions of their forefathers. It was for this reason that Jeremiah was using the illustration of Jehonadab's family and their faithfulness; read Jeremiah 35:12-16. When we read the eternal list of the faithful Jehonadab's family will be there, but will yours?

One of my favorite stories of faithfulness doesn't come from the human race, but from a shepherd dog in Edinburg, Scotland (I was able in 2003 to see the monument erected to honor this dog's faithfulness) that keep a vigil at his master's grave for 12 years after his master's death, until the dog finally died. Now for the $64,000 question, who lead this family to God? I am convinced that either Elijah or Elisha, the only two spiritual giants in that age, could have directed this family into a dedicated following of Jehovah. Remember, Elijah was told that during the reign of Ahab and Jezebel seven thousand hadn't bowed down to Baal (I Kings 19:18); was the Rechabite family numbered among them? And if not Elijah then the testimony of Elisha and the fulfillment of Elijah's prophecy about the family of Ahab might have been the one that motivated Jehonadab to side with Jehu. As in many of these illustrates, we can't be sure other than it did happen!

# 49

## WON: PHEBE THE CENCHREAN
## BY: Romans 16:1–2

I commend unto you Phebe our sister, which is a servant of the church which is at Cenchrea. That ye receive her in the Lord, as becometh saints, and that ye assist her in whatsoever business she hath need of you: for she hath been a succourer of many, and of myself also.

## ONE: PAUL

DON'T YOU THINK IT is about time we men recognize the women for the service they give to the Church of God? Because of the great surge in the Feminist Movement over the last few decades on our society it seems that most of the spiritual writers feel the only way to counter this liberal movement is to minimize and put down and ignore the gender! I think it is about time we try the Biblical approach which is to condemn the unrighteous (Revelation 2:20- Notwithstanding I have a few things against thee, because thou sufferest that woman Jezebel, which calleth herself a prophetess, to teach and to seduce my servants to commit fornication, and to eat things sacrificed unto idols.) and commend the righteous, and to illustrate all the faithful women of the Church I have chosen the Lady Phebe and what Paul said in his letter to the Romans in the verses I have printed above! This is all we know about the godly lady from Cenchrea, but is enough to know as Paul was ending his epistle to the Romans that he recognized Phebe for her service to him and the Church. I don't know when Phebe was 'won by one', but I do feel the one was Paul, for Paul was instrumental in leading so many, men or women, to the Christ!

It was Henry Bosch who related this story in one of his "Our Daily Bread" articles, and I quote: "When a Bible teacher was asked what his favorite portion of the scriptures was he replied, 'It's the last chapter of Romans!' His questioner looked it up and then explained to his surprise: 'How strange, it's mostly a collection of names!' 'Yes,' said the teacher with a smile, 'That's why I like it. The ones mentioned there are all different personalities yet each had his own specific contribution to make. The Holy Spirit had their names recorded to let us know they were individually loved and appreciated by the Lord." Many don't, but I have come to realize that if it wasn't for the Phebes of the Christian Church, work as we know it in the Body of Christ would cease. It is about time to begin to honor these unsung heroines of the faith for their contributions to the Cause of Christ; they have for too long been ignored by most because in their unselfish ways they have preferred to remain behind the scenes rather than upfront. They have chosen like Phebe to be more faithful than famous. I see three important things about Phebe in these two verses; each ought to be a part of the "Won by One' experience, whether the 'won' or the 'one'! Take time to honor the Phebe in your life and Church won't you?

First, Phebe was a SISTER. Paul's use of this word reveals just how much Phebe meant to him. It is a term of Christian endearment. It speaks of the spiritual union we have with one another. Paul and Phebe were brother and sister in the Lord: "The elder women as mothers; the younger as sisters, with all purity." (I Timothy 5:2) I feel Paul's greatest teaching on this is found in Galatians 3:28: "There is neither Jew nor Greek, there is neither bond nor free, there is neither male nor female: for ye are all one in Christ Jesus." This fighting between men and women in the Church is a sign of spiritual immaturity, not masculine domination and feminine submission. Maybe it would do each of us good if we would step back a minute and look at the women in our life and the men in our life in this light of 'brothers and sisters'! Maybe, just maybe, this 'armed camp' syndrome in the Church would finally be put to rest, once and for all?

Second, Phebe was a SERVANT. Phebe wasn't just a servant of the Church of Christ, but she was also a servant at the local Church of Cenchrea. Cenchrea was a seaport for the city of Corinth and was located on the Sardonic Gulf. Paul and Phebe probably meet on Paul's third missionary journey, and it was probably then that Paul lead Phebe to Christ: "And Paul *after this* tarried *there* yet a good while, and then took his leave of the brethren, and sailed thence into Syria, and with him Priscilla and Aquila;

having shorn *his* head in **Cenchrea**: for he had a vow." (Acts 18:18) In my over 50 years as a pastor I can't imagine what my four churches would have been like without the faithful women that served them. I have come to believe that if Christ made men the backbone of His Church then the rest of the body are women! Women teach, organize, clean, supervise, and do the hundred other things that keeps a local church going. And Paul admonition I believe is not only for the people of his day but ours: '. . .that ye receive her in the Lord as becometh saints. . ." This masculine/feminine feud in the Church hasn't been very saintly lately. God adds to His Church daily (Acts 2:47) and that addition is male and female!

Third, Phebe was a SUCCOURER. This is the Greek word 'prostatis' which means 'to be a friend or helper'. Some feel like Lydia of Philippi (Acts 16:14) that Phebe was a businesswoman. If so, Phebe like Lydia was in a great position to help Paul and others financially. Jesus had such women on his support staff: "And Joanna the wife of Chuza Herod's steward, and Susanna, and many others, **which ministered unto him of their substance.**" (Luke 8:3) Paul said that Phebe had not only helped him but many others. Others feel that Phebe was on a business trip to Rome and that Paul used her to get his letter to the Romans to Rome. We are not sure what 'business' Paul was referring too, but whatever it was Paul encouraged the readers of his letter to help her; Paul was honoring Phebe as a friend and a helper to all. Maybe it is the mothering instinct of the women that compiles them to look after the needs of other: whether the pastor or the pauper, whether the boss or the battered woman, whether the drunk or the drug addict, whether the child or the cancer victim. Just think of the last time you were in some need. Who was it a man or a woman who first knocked on your door? Who was it that assisted you in your hour of need, male or female? Who came to you that time, the deacon or the deaconess? Who meant more to you in that crisis, the pastor or the pastor's wife? Be honest! I praise the Lord for the Phebe that lived in my house for 48 year; my dear wife Coleen who in her life impacted more people in this way than me. It was the Psalmist that wrote: "Blessed *is* he that considereth the poor: the Lord will deliver him in time of trouble." (Psalm 41:1) How women consider more the needs of others than we men. For that reason and so many more we need to honor the women of our lives or the women of the Church just like Paul did when he thought of all those people (33 names) mentioned in Romans 16, but when he pondered who to mention first he write down Phebe, a woman!

May we start today cleaning up our relationship with our sisters in Christ. May we see their service to their God as beneficial to the Cause of Christ. Deep down we know that we can't do this great work without them, just like they can't do it without us. Christ has joined us together, to work together for the common good of His Church, so let us stop bickering and let us start being a blessing to those who really need our help. Won by One includes women: "For we are labourers together with God. . ." (I Corinthians 3:9)

# 50

**WON**: TABITHA THE JOPPAITE
**BY**: Acts 9:36

Now there was at Joppa a certain disciple named Tabitha, which by interpretation is called Dorcas: this woman was full of good works and almsdeeds which she did.

**ONE**: ONLY GOD KNOWS

I KNOW THAT MANY of the individuals highlighted in this "Won by One" fall into the category of who actually lead them to a saving knowledge of Jesus; some underlined are very clear and the others I have shared who I believe was the instrument God used to their salvation. I decided to share my last example with this verse in Acts 2:47 being the 'one': "**. . .And the Lord added to the church daily such as should be saved."** Ultimately it is God who is the dominate 'one' in our 'won by one' philosophy, but God's eternal plan was always to use people to work out, fulfill His final purpose no matter the situation, including evangelization. With that settled, I would like to give you one more amazing example, a personal favorite, the lady Tabitha of Joppa.

What do you consider God's work? For most of us it is things like preaching, teaching, mission's work, evangelism, and helping the poor. How many of us would put sewing on that list? I hope after you read this 'won by one' devotional that sewing will be on your list of God ordained works and that sewing will be near the top of that list. If that happens, it will all be because of an early disciple named Tabitha, or Dorcas. Actually both names mean 'gazelle' with Tabitha being the Hebrew name and

Dorcas the Greek name. As one of the old writers explained it: "It suited her well, for she was not only swift to run errands of mercy, but she performed her good works gracefully. Her faithful devotion to the Saviour in commonplace things and her compassion for her friends and neighbors made her a model Christian!" Her full story is recorded by Luke in Acts 9:36–42, and it brings to light a ministry that is almost extinct today, a ministry that once was a primary ministry of the Church (Acts 6:1–2), but now the government agencies on aging takes care of most of the widows. Paul makes a point in I Timothy 5 to instruct the Church in this ministry, but instead of being responsibly most Christian families simply deposit their widows in some care facility, and when there is no family and the Church is supposed to care for them they don't. Read carefully I Timothy 5:3–16! In Joppa things were different; they followed Paul's rules about widows because living there was Tabitha. Tabitha was always ready to help even if it meant sewing a dress or fixing a pair of pants, and not until Tabitha's untimely death is it brought to light just how important and vital Tabitha was to the people of Joppa; especially the widows.

Tabitha seemingly was a seamstress by trade, or maybe just a lady with skills in sewing? Whichever the case Tabitha used her ability to help others, and probably her story wouldn't make the modern ministry magazines today, but her death sent a shockwave through the Christian community of Joppa to the point they rushed off a messenger to Lydda where the Apostle Peter was staying and asked if he might come. I to have come to believe that most churches can survive a while without a pastor, a deacon or two, and a Sunday school superintendent, but few local churches will last long without a Dorcas! So many in the Church today want the lofty positions; few aspire to the widow's ministry. Have we become so far removed from the early Church that people like Tabitha are not needed, and if they are in the Church not recognized for the important serves they provide to the most fragile among us? Again if you read Acts 6 you will see that after evangelism and ministry in the Word helping the widows was seen as God ordained, and we are not talking about a fruit basket at Christmas, or a visit once a year, but a daily care program for each widow, the modern Church ought to be ashamed!

Luke records that when Peter arrived he resurrected the dead saint: "And he gave her *his* hand, and lifted her up, and when he had called the saints and widows, presented her alive." (Acts 9:41) This humble member of the local church of Joppa was given back to the church to continue her labors of mercy and love. This Biblical story reminds me of a poem I read long ago: "I asked the Lord to let me do some mighty work for Him, to fight amidst His battle hosts, then sing the victor's hymn. I longed my ardent love to show, but Jesus would not have it so. He placed me in a quiet home, whose life was calm and still, and gave me little things to do, my daily rounds to fill; I could not think it good to be just put aside so silently. So as I thought my prayer unheard, I asked the Lord once more that He would give me work for Him, and open wide the door; forgetting that my Master knew just what was best for me to do. Then quietly the answer came, my child I heard thy cry, think not that mighty deeds alone will bring the victory; the battle has been planned by Me, let daily thy conquest be!" So many today are only out to make a living, not a difference; to see what our occupation can get us; not what our occupation can be used for to the helping of others. The true measure of making a life and a living is in what we give, not get (Acts 20:35) and in Dorcas we have a godly example to emulate. God saves people to place them in His body where they can best serve the fellowship; it is far more important to be found faithful than famous, just like Tabitha!

Today as you read this story about Dorcas take stock of the gift or gifts the Good Lord has given you (Ephesians 4:8). Am I using my ability to sew to help others? Am I using my skill as a carpenter, a cook, or an electrician to help others? In my over fifty years in the pastorate I can't tell you a trade that I haven't seen being used for the Lord's work, and so many of those skilled people have helped widows; like fixing their car, mending a fence, and doing their taxes. I have spent a lifetime visiting widows (James 1:27) and have often asked this question: if you should die today how many widows will show up to your funeral? Remember Paul's last admonition in his widow's challenge: "If any man or woman that believeth have widows, let them relieve them, and let not the church be charged; that it may relieve them that are widows indeed." (I Timothy 5:16) Remember one of Jesus' last exhortations to His disciples: "...Verily I say unto you, Inasmuch as ye have done *it* unto one of the least of these my brethren, ye have done *it* unto me." (Matthew 25:40) I am not saying that only the widows need help, for I think you know that I am only using the neglected widow as the example of the many that are being ignored by the Church. Someday your candle will burn low and flicker into the night of death: what kind of life will you be known for? May the challenge of the people of Joppa to Peter be taken into consideration: "Then Peter arose and went with them. When he was come, they brought him into the upper chamber: and all the widows stood by him weeping, and shewing the coats and garments which Dorcas made, while she was with them." (Acts 9:39) What kind of kindness have you been showing the widows or anybody else lately? It is time we consider the importance of people like Dorcas.

Who won Dorcas to the Lord I know not, but this I know, that unknown individual helped the vunderable to a better life in Christ; we could do far worst in our service!

# OF ALL NATIONS

WE HAVE COME TO the end of our look into the concept of 'won by one', but I have a few more thoughts I would like to share from Revelation 7:9-10: "After this I beheld, and, lo, a great multitude, which no man could number, **of all nations**, and **kindreds**, and **people**, and **tongues**, stood before the throne, and before the Lamb, clothed with white robes, and palms in their hands; and cried with a loud voice, saying, ***Salvation*** to our God which sitteth upon the throne, and unto the Lamb." Isn't it interesting that one of the final messages of that heavenly song is 'salvation'! On that we might recognize and understand that still the greatest mission in this world is the reality of 'Won by One'!

In our attempt to highlight and underline the Biblical principle of 'won by one', we have also tried to share the scriptural precept of 'out of every'. As you have noticed I have deliberately chosen different people groups and different races in this series of devotionals to reveal the amazing concept that God's grace and salvation would eventually reach at least one representative from 'every' and 'all' nations and now I believe 'tribes' after my sixth trip to India to visit some tribal ministries in Chhattisgarh and Kerala states: "And then shall appear the sign of the Son of man in heaven: and then shall ***all the tribes of the earth*** mourn, and they shall see the Son of man coming in the clouds of heaven with power and great glory." (Matthew 24:30) Large people groups like the Chinese and Russians will be there, but so will the small tribes like the Bhatra and Dhruwa people of Chhattisgarh will be there as well. Even though all the people from all the nations and all the people from all the tribes will be saved, Jesus died for all and that will be seen in the representatives around the Throne of God: "And he is the propitiation for our sins: and not for ours only, but also for **the sins of the whole world**." (I John 2:2) I like this out of Paul's famous sermon on Mars' Hill: "And hath made of one blood all nations of men for to dwell on all the face of the earth, and hath determined the times before appointed, and the bounds of their habitation; that **they should seek the Lord**, if haply they might feel after him, and find him, though he be not far from every one of us." (Acts 17:26-27) This is the same message from Peter to Cornelius that I have made reference to so many times in this book: "Then Peter opened *his* mouth, and said, Of a truth I perceive that God is no respecter of persons: but **in every nation he that feareth him**, and worketh righteousness, is accepted with him." (Acts 10:34-35)

God has always had a world-wide heart for the lost; not just for the Jews! I will be honest that I missed for years this concept clearly stated by Jesus in His sermon on the Mount Olivet: "And this gospel of the kingdom shall be preached in all the world for a witness unto **all nations**; and then shall the end come." (Matthew 24:14) For years, I preached and proclaimed we were seeking the last person to be saved, to be added by the Lord to His Body (Acts 2:47), but in reality we are seeking the last representative to the last nation or tribe. I have become convinced that 'all the nations' have been reached, but it is the often overlooked, the '. . .kindreds and people, and tongues. . .' that still need to be reached. There are still hundreds in India alone, and that is why I have been stirred (II Timothy 1:7) to help those who are seeking the representative from the isolated and ignored tribes to be reached. The work is being done in India as well as other places around the world; we just need to keep at it, for I don't believe the Lord will be back until His complete commission is done, and that includes the tribes of the world!

Mrs. Charles Cowman in her classic devotional 'Springs in the Valley' gives, in my opinion, the greatest description of this future gathering, when she wrote:

> "What a scene of unimaginable grandeur that will be, when at last all nations are gathered to His feet! That will include representatives from all the European States, from Iceland to the far north to Greece in the south, and from Portugal in the west to hidden (wrote during the iron curtain days) saint in Soviet Russia in the east. There will be many from Algeria, Morocco, and the Atlas Mountains; from Egypt and the Nile Valley; from the sandy deserts and the mountains of the Sahara; from the great lakes in central Africa, from the banks of the Niger, the Calabar, the Congo, and the Zambesi Rivers; from the uplands of South Africa. There will be gathered to Christ many from Palestine, Transjordan, and Arabia; India will contribute her millions; and even the closed

lands like Nepal, Sikkim and Tibet, Christ will gather His own. From the islands of the Dutch East Indies they will come: Java, Sumatra, Bali, Celebes, Lombok, Soembawa, Borneo, and the rest, and will be gathered at the feet of the Redeemer. From the teeming millions of central Asia, from China, Japan, Korea (she didn't know about North and South, but I believe both will supply their representatives), Manchukuo and Mongolia, there will be an immense home-going to the Saviour. From the myriad islands of the Pacific the peoples of Polynesia and Melanesia will be gathered to the Lord who redeemed them. From Australia and New Zealand there will be multitudes who will join in the glad song of praise. From every republic of Central, South, and North America and from the West Indies islands: Cuba (she wouldn't know about Castro), Haiti, Jamaica, Porto Rico, and the lesser Antilles, they will come. From the far-off forests and lakes of Canada there will be a similar home-going. Whether the tongues be those of the white race, or of the red, or the black, the gathering to Christ will be overwhelmingly splendid!"

To this modern mass of people groups will come the myriad of nations from the past; long since extinct and gone: the Semites, the Gittites, the Amorites, the Midianites, the Moabites, the Hittites, the Canaanites, the Gibeonites, and the Ammonites and all the others that I don't know anything about but God hasn't missed a one in His gathering of the nations. They will be numbered with the Phoenicians, the Macedonians, the Cyrenians, the Babylonians, the Italians, the Galileans, the Ethiopians, and the Medians. Past and present mingled together in a mighty chorus of praise and thanksgiving for the 'salvation of the Lord'!

I will end with this from the pen of Paul and a poem that has blessed me for years; first this scripture from Paul's epistle to the Romans: "Even us, whom he hath called, not of the Jews only, but also of the Gentiles? As he saith also in Hosea, I will call them my people, which were not my people; and her beloved, which was not beloved. And it shall come to pass, *that* in the place where it was said unto them, ye *are* not my people; there shall they be called the children of the living God." (Romans 9:24–26) Amen! And from an unknown poet these stirring words:

> "From earth's wide bounds, from ocean's farthest coast, through gates of pearl stream in countless hosts, singing to the Father, Son, and Holy Ghost, Hallelujah!"

What a day that will be and I have made reservations through the shed blood of Jesus Christ to be there; numbered among the Maineaics that have placed their hope and trust in our Lord and Saviour Jesus Christ. Could I ask what nation, tribe, kindred, tongue, or people you will be representing on that grand and glorious day?

www.ingramcontent.com/pod-product-compliance
Lightning Source LLC
Chambersburg PA
CBHW051050160426
43193CB00010B/1138